Shazia
In

Carol
x x

Memoirs
of a
Feminist Mother

Carol Fox

Ringwood Publishing
Glasgow

First published in Scotland in 2015
by
Ringwood Publishing
7 Kirklee Quadrant, Glasgow G12 0TS
www.ringwoodpublishing.com
e-mail mail@ringwoodpublishing.com

ISBN 978-1-901514-21-6

British Library Cataloguing-in Publication Data

A catalogue record for this book is available from the British
Library

Typeset in Times New Roman 11

Printed and bound in the UK
by Lonsdale Direct Solutions

For

NATASHA
and her siblings,
Simone and Elliott,

Single parents everywhere who do their very best.

And with loving thanks to my parents for their support and perseverance.

Prologue

To my precious daughter,

It has taken me a long time to write this story. I want to tell you about my quest to bring you into this world. As you set out on your own path in life, it is important that you understand how much you were wanted and how much you are loved. As your favourite children's story says, "*You are loved to the moon and back.*" The world is such a better place with you here. Already you are full of hopes, dreams and ambitions to do well but also to do some good in the world. You are my pride and joy.

I look at you as you dazzle and impress and I ask myself every day, '*How is it possible that I was blessed to have such a wonderful daughter?*'

Some might say that God had little to do with our story. Indeed, many have. Our story owes nothing to religious folk who believe that women should lead narrow, proscribed lives of self-sacrifice and caring for others. As feminists, we have to be eternally mindful and always grateful to the women who have gone before us. Generations of women who had the courage to challenge and broaden our life choices.

Yet centuries later the same debate still rages about whether women can have 'it' all? Without, it seems to me, much real inquiry as to what 'it' means.

This elusive 'it' is your life. I fought so hard to give you life. You have the absolute right to stride forth now and positively determine your own future. Of course, at times, you will be uncertain and you will need all your courage to overcome your own doubts and the anxieties of others around you. That's okay. All choices involve doubt and risk. Listen to good people, accept wise counsel, grasp opportunities and overcome disappointments. And, at the end of every day take a deep breath. Look calmly in the mirror and make sure you can smile because you are in charge of your life and you like the person smiling back at you.

Life can be hard. You may face obstacles and tough choices. I hope you continue to enjoy rude health, face few heartbreaks and experience more happiness than sadness in your adult life. Your moral compass will help you to make the right choices for you. Your feminism will give you the strength to keep going in the face of adversity, opposition and sadness. It is truly amazing what the human spirit can endure. Be brave and trust your instincts.

I have persevered over the years to record our story. To be truthful, until recently, it is perhaps more my story than yours. I want to tell you the full story in all its splendid glory. When I was young, born to reject conventional wisdom and the established, well-trodden path, I caused daily anxiety and consternation by just waking up each day and questioning the reality around me. Fortunately, for you and your generation of young women, that reality has changed massively. You have more choices and opportunities than ever before.

Let's be clear though that your life choices did not happen as if by magic. They did not evolve through time alone, nor were they benevolently handed down from on high from a benign God or patriarch. Change has only ever arisen from the determination, spirit, courage and hard work of generations of women: mothers, grannies, aunties, sisters, married women, single women, single parents and other un-biddable and unclassifiable women. It is your time to decide how you want to live your life, in whatever order or form you choose. You can go out into the wide world with the support of your mother, your grandmother and your long gone feminist sisters who fought for your rights.

You deserve it all.

Chapter 1

Dearest Daughter,

The first time it happened, I was exactly the age you are now. I had just graduated from university with the world at my feet but another part of my anatomy was about to malfunction and determine the course of my life.

It was summer 1981. Everyone's attention was focused upon the Royal Wedding, as Lady Diana Spencer prepared to marry her prince. The shops were full of royal wedding tea sets which sensible Scottish people didn't buy. I had little interest in weddings, royal or otherwise. Born in 1961 and the same age as Diana, I had a passing sympathy for a posh girl who did not seem very bright. *'Poor Diana,'* I thought, *'if only she had discovered feminism.'*

My first degree from Glasgow University was in maths but unusually I was turned down by teacher training college. Perhaps they sensed that I did not have a burning ambition to be a maths teacher, but I think it had more to do with my lifelong inability to bite my tongue. I had pitched up for an interview at the Catholic teacher training college, called Notre Dame, in Glasgow. I really should have known better but all my university friends were applying and if I wanted to apply to the non-denominational alternative, I had to get special permission from the bishop or write to the Pope or some such thing which, at the time, just seemed like too much trouble.

So why was I turned down? Truth was that I just wasn't a very good Catholic. I hadn't had much to do with the bishop or the chapel since my first holy communion age six when I was dressed as a diminutive bride, or my confirmation when I was about eight and I proudly took the confirmation name of Theresa, just so that I could keep the same initials as my big brother, your Uncle Colin. We had been sent to a Catholic school merely to keep the peace and avoid the wrath of Nellie,

3

my matriarchal grandmother, your great grandmother.

Here we are on those important holy days, smiling for the camera, doing the right thing by my Granny and the Pope. My grandmother looks so proud in her posh coats and chapel hats. For reasons of economy, when we finally reached my confirmation after the completion of the new St Brendan's chapel, I was squeezed into the same dress as I wore at my communion but Nellie was pleased with her new hat, reassured that her first granddaughter was paraded to the world as a good Catholic. Besides a clean house that's all that really mattered to her.

Ever practical, my mum refused to buy me a new pair of white shoes just for one day. The dress fitted but by then was shorter than the bishop would have liked. I remember my mum getting the toolbox out from the hall cupboard and using a screwdriver to unscrew the taps from my white tap dancing shoes. She whitened them and added a new white ribbon. So I tapped my way down the aisle without a thought for my eternal soul, more concerned that my second hand feet were lowering the tone of the occasion.

First Communion and Confirmation

Remember when you were young, you called your great grandmother 'Nana in the sky', not because she was dead, but because she lived on the fourteenth floor of a council tower block in Motherwell? You were such a bright wee thing, even then. You used to say things like that all the time which made me laugh. Like the time in the park, when you were in your buggy and we passed a poodle and you asked, '*Mummy why is that dog wearing bunches*?' Clever and funny, that's you.

It wasn't so funny when you were only about four and you accidentally knocked the head off one of 'Nana in the sky's' holy statues. It was only cheap plaster of paris, most probably from a chapel jumble sale, but it was her favourite tearful Holy Mary statue which had sat on her dressing table for years. We picked Mary's head up off the carpet and tried to glue it back together. The way Nellie went on, you would think you had killed the mother of God herself, so you were scared to go back and visit her after that. Although she was my only granny, I'm afraid she just wasn't a very nice person. She didn't like anyone on the television with red hair because she called them blue nose Rangers' supporters. Even when I was small, I didn't understand why the colour of someone's nose or hair made her so mad.

But looking back, it seems to me that my only granny was always angry. Maybe she had good reason. She never seemed happy to have been a mother of five, and later on she was definitely not pleased to be a granny when we came along. At fifty-one, she insisted upon the title of 'Nana' which sounded warm and lovable. But there was a terror about her, a feeling that the anger she stocked up might just lash out at you, at an unpredictable moment on the bus or in the Co-op when she was giving her dividend number to the girl at the till. *25327.* I used to rehearse the number in my head just in case. She sometimes lashed out with her hands, especially if my talking and asking questions got too much for her and I was forgetting my place – children to be seen and not heard. More frequently the anger came from the bite of her tongue. Her morning visits to chapel and to confession must have been her daily dose of anger management or sixties-style counselling. When I went with her to mass as a child, I was marched along, black lacy mantilla on my head, with orders not to open my mouth or else she would give me something to cry about.

5

I can laugh now, as I look back at the sixties outfits that I modelled as I was initiated into the Catholic faith every Sunday morning. My mum was a good knitter but that mustard knitted Arran pattern dress was a step too far. Then, there was the yellow and black MacLeod tartan trouser suit. Oh, God.

My mum had somehow managed to get hold of a bale of this loud tartan material. She then asked a family friend called Lottie, who was famous for being very good with a sewing machine, to make me the trouser suit. Lottie didn't have any children of her own, but she had a niece who entered ballroom dancing competitions and wore sparkly dresses with underskirts and sequins. When we went for fittings to Lottie's house for my tartan trouser suit, I sensed sadness from my mum as she looked at me and sighed, knowing I was just not a sparkly frock or tartan trouser suit type of girl. Even though my mum worked, she was determined to live up to her mother's standards and so she outsourced the more creative aspects of motherhood. What an outfit, in yellow and black tartan. There was a bit of material left over so Lottie finished off her creation with a flourish, producing an original black and yellow cowboy hat with a large brim, a flap at one side pinned up with a brooch and ribbons with a large bow underneath my chin. I remember everyone looking at me sitting at mass with my 'more Catholic than thou' Nana and my yellow and black tartan cowboy hat. I wasn't sure if they were jealous of my new suit or just my hat. I told myself I was the bee's knees, proud to be different, or at least determined not to let any embarrassment show.

I have searched high and low for a photo of me in my tartan ensemble, but couldn't find one. What I did find was a photo of me looking every bit like Little Red Riding Hood with a bun. In fact, I remember going to school with curlers in my hair and a scarf around my head on more than one occasion such were the pressures to keep up appearances. In this photo I look like a miniature of my mum with her bun and hand knitted Arran cardigan.

Little Red Riding Hood and my Mum with bun

Going to mass at that time was something of a fashion parade, where the procession to the altar for holy communion was accompanied by unchristian comments from my Nana, *'Look at the state of her, that coat has seen better days / is too tight / is not suitable for the chapel.'* or if the coat was actually lovely and expensive looking, *'Who does she think she is, with her nose in the air? Knew her when she was nothing, no better than she should be.'* Then later on, everyone would turn and shake hands offering each other the sign of the peace, shaking hands with the posh coat lady, my granny smiling might say, *'May peace be with you.'* It was all too confusing. Luckily, I was not the only one not making much sense of what was going on with the adults all around me as I can share my memories with my brother. Colin also has his tales of woe as an altar boy fainting in the middle of mass and being carried out in an 'over-the-shoulder' fireman's lift by the St Vincent de Paul helpers. Going to mass in our family was not an uneventful affair but for me, it had little to do with communing with God. It was our duty and besides, the teacher would go round the class every Monday morning and ask which mass you had attended and you got into serious trouble if you either missed mass or hadn't been to the earliest service. While the religious messages may have passed me by, the routine of attending mass every Sunday in my spectacular outfits and trying to make sense of Catholic education left me with a very thick skin and an enquiring mind.

Some of my earliest memories around five are of living in Germany, in a block of flats in a small town called Celle amongst forces families. This interlude in our otherwise normal Scottish childhood arose after a holiday to visit my aunt and uncle turned into a nine month stay, with us being sent to the Army school while my dad returned home after two weeks. I remember the flat had a long hallway which encouraged racing around and there was a dense forest across the street which we four cousins played in for hours. It was a freer and easier time, at least for my brother and me, if not for my parents.

I remember to this day, age five, arriving at the new school in Germany when my brother and I stood, holding hands in a corridor, just the two of us, for what seemed like an age. It had been time for religious assembly and all the other kids had long since disappeared into different rooms. When finally a teacher asked us why we were still standing in the corridor, my brother explained that we did not know where to go. The teacher then said that the Roman Catholics had to go to room five, but Colin replied in a loud concerned voice, *'But miss, we are not Roman Catholics, we are Scottish Catholics.'* I was less bothered about what type of five year old Catholic I was meant to be, but I *was* worried about whether I might get the belt for talking in this new school like in Scotland. To my delight there was no belt.

We spent Christmas 1966 in Germany. St Nicholas came on a camel to the school and gave out strange big brown cube sweets dusted with brown icing sugar. Nothing like that had ever happened in Scotland. At home in Motherwell, we had

8

been into the big shops in Glasgow to queue to see Santa but there was no camel. On my sixth birthday in Germany in January 1967, I was so pleased to get a real pine wooden sledge. Then all the snow disappeared the very next day.

Being with so many English children, I developed quite a posh English accent which, despite expensive elocution lessons, did not survive the return to Scotland later that year. There is a photograph of me age six and my brother aged seven on a day out in Germany when we visited Bergen Belsen concentration camp. My young memories of that day are of racing around between buildings and statues playing hide and seek with my brother and cousins. The true adult backdrop to those nine months abroad was never explained but shortly after we returned home we finally qualified for a bigger council house with a back and front door and a bedroom each for me and Colin. Until then our family of four had been living in a one bedroom flat while we were on the council's waiting list for the treasured back and front door.

My first home was a council flat in Wishaw, which was my dad's home with his elderly grandparents. He had been almost orphaned when he was three when his mother, aged only twenty-three had died of TB and his father was in the army, sent to Singapore and becoming one of the first Japanese prisoners of war. As a result, my Dad was brought up by his maternal grandparents who were already elderly pensioners in their seventies and had no money to look after him. They went to the parish to ask for assistance and were told that he was '*His faither's problem,*' even though his father was half dead on the other side of the world.

No welfare state then, so they made the best of things, cutting up old coats to make rugs to sell and getting by on food rations. His granny showed him how to knit and sew. He might have been the cleverest boy in the class but there was no money to keep him at school. When I was young he always told me the story of the first day he met his dad when he finally

9

came home, and turned up many years later unannounced at the school with a banana. It had been the very first time he had ever seen a banana. He was determined that when he grew up his family would have a good education and enough money to enjoy bananas every day of the week. But his own upbringing without parents or siblings had perhaps not prepared him for the demands of family life. His role above all else was to be the breadwinner and to provide us with the best education possible as a route out of his poverty. He worked long hours and as he established his own new family, we were all crammed into the same council flat of his childhood.

*

I remember we had a long path down to the road and a fence which I regularly climbed to escape. We lived across the road from the McCrumb twins. These boys regularly took it upon themselves to batter my big brother. Then they gloated, laughing as he walked home crying to our mum. My brother was five and they were six. He did not stand a chance but then he didn't really try to fight back. A blonde, fat and placid baby he had grown into a dark haired, good natured and well behaved little boy who did not like fighting. Truth was that in Scottish terms my big brother was just a wee bit soft. To this day he is good humoured and hates conflict.

One particular day I watched him open our gate and walk up our path crying. I was sitting on the doorstep making chalk marks on the slabs, drawing faces and trying to write my name. As he approached me, I stood up and threw down my packet of coloured chalk which fell in pieces to the ground. I put my arm round him and told him I would look after him. '*Who hit ye son, who hit ye?*' I sat him on the door step still crying. Then like a bullet, I turned and ran straight down our path, out of our gate, across the road, over their fence and up their path towards those two still laughing boys. I summoned up all my strength, punched one right in the face then pummelled my fists into the stomach of the other stunned brother. Then,

10

running as fast as I could back to our house, I shouted to Colin to run fast and open the front door quick.

My mum opened the door in response to our banging and shouting and we fell into the hall. I slammed the door behind us, stood with my back to the door in amongst the coats hanging on the hook above and waited for more banging fists. My heart was beating fast. It felt powerful and dangerous. My brother had by then stopped crying but he looked at me bewildered about what I had done and scared about what was going to happen next.

There was a knock on our door a short time later. This time the twins had gone crying to their mother. There she was on our doorstep, red faced and arms folded. My mum calmly opened our door as I hid behind her legs while my brother hung further back down the hall. My mum listened politely to the complaint about me being a menace to the neighbourhood and hitting her two boys. I tried to push my way past my mother's legs to tell the true story but she held me back and politely replied that she did not need any lessons on how to bring up her children from Mrs McCrumb, thank you very much, and closed the door. My mum was a nurse and had a job and children. She was confident about how she performed both her roles. She did not bother that much about what the neighbours said.

But that day my mother looked at my brother hiding shyly further down the hall. She smiled, encouraging him towards her. She then turned to me and said, *'Carol, you know it isn't ladylike to fight in the street, why don't you go and play with your dolls.'* My brother looked a bit sheepish, sorry that I was getting a row. But I could tell that mum was not really that angry. Obediently, for once, I spent the rest of that afternoon playing with my dolls, wondering when I would see the McCrumb twins again and hoping that this time they would be scared of me.

We went to Germany and then moved house when we came back so I never saw those twins again. Our move back

11

also involved another change of school and I can take myself instantly back to the first day at St Brendans R.C. Primary School in Motherwell. We arrived wearing our old green blazers to be met by a mob of kids completely in brown from head to toe. Needless to say my talking and the belting at this new school continued apace. I was clever and in the top set but I was wilful, unlike any other girl in my class. I really tried hard to do girly things like swapping scraps and skipping but it was boring. Before the advent of computer games or sophisticated children, playtime at school revolved around a few gender segregated activities. The girls who wore pigtails, ribbons and lots of clasps or bows in their hair did not want to get dirty or messy so they would sit in a small group at the far end of the yard on a low wall and swap their scraps. This was the feminine currency of the day. Each week at the local newsagents these girls spent their pocket money on sheets of paper scraps. They were sold in colourful single sheets covered in clear plastic with each picture joined together by a small strip of paper. You could buy pages of flowers or angels or babies or dresses. You could buy a paper doll and then paper clothes to cover the paper doll. Some girls cut them up and stuck the scraps in a special scrapbook with extra thick cardboard pages to cope with the glue. Others kept them in an old biscuit tin so that you could take it to school for playtime. The sheets of scraps always had doublers and so at playtime the girls would swap their doublers. The most popular scraps were the fat angels who sat on clouds or the scraps with glitter, but they were more expensive so were worth at least two angels or four flowers.

This activity amused many girls of my generation each lunchtime and playtime. I tried to like it but I could not work out what I did with the scraps once I had managed to get two sparkly angels for my flowers. What did they do exactly, except look nice? It all seemed a bit pointless to me. So I decided to stop buying scraps, spent my pocket money on sweets instead and played with the boys.

The boys ran around the yard like possessed heathens every playtime. Maybe it was a reaction to the strict discipline of a sixties Catholic primary school, sitting with arms folded for long periods, listening to and repeating stories from the Catechism and getting the belt if you had not learned your holy stories properly. I got the belt one day when the teacher asked the class, *'What is the name of the strong man in the Bible?'* I raised my hand first and said in a loud voice, *'Please Miss, Tarzan.'* I thought I was clever but she thought I was being cheeky and the rest of the class fell silent and didn't risk an answer themselves as I got the belt, *again*. When the bell rang and the doors opened, the boys ran around the playground as fast as they could and made as much noise as possible. One of the favourite boys' games was 'tig' where you had to run after someone and catch them, then they were 'it' and they had to run and catch someone else until the bell rang. I can't remember how it evolved but a few of us girls, bored with swapping scraps, wanted to join in with the boys and play tig. Our rules were that when you caught a boy they had to decide whether they wanted a kiss, a cuddle or torture. My preferred option was always torture, and so I raced around the playground with evil intent. Of course, I also received my own share of torture, usually a Chinese burn or bending fingers as far back as they could go but I also learned to run fast. Despite the pain it was much more fun than swapping scraps.

After school, when our homework was done and we had finished our dinner, we could go outside to play in the street. A small gang of us would hang about our scheme, trying to keep ourselves amused. There was a swing park close by and a grassy area where ball games were permitted, so each evening started off with these permissible activities. As it grew darker and we grew bored, someone always suggested we play chap door, run away. Then there was a system for egging each other on, who was going to be the leader, who was going to open the gate, who was going to actually chap the door, who got to do it last time? So as the adults in the street settled down

13

to watch Coronation Street, we would time the knock at the door to maximum effect. By the time the door was opened, we were half way down the street, giggling and hiding behind the hedges. Except one night full of bravado, we went too far and chapped too many doors at the same time. I remember crouching behind a neighbour's hedge, when this large arm descended and grabbed me by the neck of my jumper. I was frogmarched to my front door while my gang of so called friends ran away fast in the opposite direction. I was mortified. I thought I was much too clever to get caught. But there I was, disgraced on my own doorstep with this man chapping very loudly on my front door. My parents were angry but I can't remember exactly what happened. I think they resolved to keep me busy either inside the house, or at organised activities. It wasn't long after that when they bought a piano and I was kept busy doing piano lessons, two nights a week at Brownies and dancing lessons on a Saturday morning. My poor parents spent loads of their hard earned money keeping me busy and out of trouble, but I remained throughout a talentless rebel.

*

My mother was a nurse in casualty. She witnessed death and tragic accidents every day of her working life. She would not allow us to have bikes or engage in any remotely dangerous activities (hence trumpet and piano lessons). I complained every Christmas and birthday that I wanted a bike and some front teeth (I knocked out all my front teeth aged four running to the ice-cream van with my hands inside a cape and didn't have any new teeth till aged eight). In time, of course, new teeth arrived but I never got that longed-for bike. Then, in an outrageous act of injustice, inequality and unforgivable cruelty, a red two-wheeler bike appeared one Christmas for my brother. I was incensed. He wheeled around smugly while I demanded explanations for the inequality of their parenting, only to be told he was older and wiser, less reckless; he would be more careful. He was a boy. Furious, I bided my time.

When the initial novelty had worn off, and he was less enthralled by his new toy (and his smug victory over me), I quietly took the bike into the garage. In those days, Blue Peter encouraged children to make things. We had a number of lamps in our house made out of old bottles of Dimple Whiskey which you covered in plaster of paris, stuck on chucky stones then painted gold before fitting a fetching shade onto the bottle base. My mum loved us enough to allow these lamps to sit proudly on her side board. That day, I found some of this leftover gold paint in the garage and daubed gold spots all over my brother's red bike so that it was too sissy for him to ride with his mates. I was triumphant only for the shortest time, as I now fell heir to this ridiculous looking bike with gold spots when the rest of the world had choppers with low seats and high handle bars. But it was the principle of the thing.

My quiet and good natured brother was fastidious about coin collecting and at one stage in his life could recite all the capital cities in the world. Quite useful training really, for a budding international Marxist. I was more out there, being an early feminist delinquent and forming rival gangs. His coin collection was my brother's pride and joy. He had an old biscuit tin with different layers of cotton wool separating the shillings, sixpences, thruppences and pennies which, he dreamed, would be worth a fortune one day. Apparently, it all depended on the year and the particular king or queen on the back. Anyway, unknown to all, I secretly raided his prized coin collection when the ice cream van came round and I had no money. I tried to take the less precious coins and spaced them all out again so that there was no obvious gaps or signs of theft. I feasted out on Curly Wurlies and packets of crisps for ages and they tasted even better with the thrill of my secret wrongdoing.

During the summer school holidays, I stayed at my grandparents because my parents were working. My Nana's days were spent cooking, cleaning the house or going to mass. That was her lot. The evenings were tense as the dinner burnt dry in the oven. After closing time, my lovely grandpa would fall into the house with beery breath, slobbery kisses and a half eaten box of chocolates. '*Here ye are sweetheart darlin' I brought ye some chocolates but I was a wee bit hungry.*' He would laugh and snort at his own jokes while trying to put his arms around her to land a big drunken kiss before she fought him off. The rest of the box of chocolates was often slammed into the back of the roaring coal fire as she went to fetch his tray and presented his spoiled dinner, muttering all the time under her breath, '*Drink is God's curse.*' Meanwhile my grandpa, plastered and hungry, would sit with a big smile on his face and the tray on his lap scoffing the burnt offerings, '*Lovely, sweetheart, just lovely,*' before he fell fast asleep, snoring in the chair in front of the coal fire. This was fairly typical of the life of most of the women in the street and was my first real insight as a young child into love and marriage. Admittedly, my mum and dad had a more civilised and well organised arrangement, where he worked days and she worked nights so all the bills were paid and we were brought up well, from a good family. Still, to me, from a young age, marriage seemed as odd as all the religion and going-to-mass palaver. Not long before she died, my Nana told me with a great sense of pride in her voice that she had never worked a day after she got married and she had never worn a swimming costume. The epitaph of a respectable working class Scottish Catholic married mother of five perhaps. But not providing much happiness on Earth it seemed.

She died when you were in primary school. We didn't go to her funeral but we went to the Rosary, when far too many people crowded into her one bedroom council flat clutching their rosary beads. Tall men in long dark overcoats were squeezed into every space, even the bathroom, saying their prayers over the cistern. You were worried about how they would get the coffin down from the forteenth floor in the lift. She always had holy water at the front door for visitors to bless themselves as they came in and out of the flat. She confessed

16

to me that when you were a baby she secretly baptised you in her own wee impromptu ceremony in her hallway while I was making a cup of tea in the kitchen. For lots of reasons, my granny definitely put me off religion and being a Catholic.

*

The experiences I have described explain why I couldn't bring myself just to do and say what was expected of a good Catholic girl. Like you, in my last year at university, I was trying to work out what to do with my life and how I could possibly pay back the previous struggles and hard work of all those generations of parents and grandparents. When I reached the dreaded interview to be a maths teacher I was asked whether I was a practising Catholic. I had long since stopped going to mass. But I was not *lapsed*. Not in the sense that I got too lazy or forgot my Catechism that had been so robustly belted into me or even that as a student I couldn't be bothered getting out of bed on a Sunday morning. No. I had rejected all the tenets of the chapel when I was around thirteen and had discovered a thing called feminism and women throwing themselves under horses to get the vote. Wonderful, I thought; that was the type of woman I was born to be. Feminism made such complete sense to me and explained all my previous struggles with the boring ladylike pursuits and so I styled myself as a latter-day suffragette.

At this crucial interview, I thought honesty was the best policy. I looked the priest in the eye and told him that I was no longer a practising Catholic but I was pleased to tell him that I was very much a practising socialist and feminist who intended to do some good in the world. All my quieter and wiser friends were accepted and went on to become teachers. Their life path was laid out; long holidays, good pension and keeping on the right side of those priests and bishops. Not me. I received a letter saying that no matter what class of degree I obtained, I was not wanted.

So at twenty, having rejected Catholicism and embraced

17

feminism with a wholehearted passion, I graduated in to the big wide world without much of an idea of a career, or any life path, other than to remain true to my socialism and feminism. I gave the Maths degree to your Nana and Papa and I set out to find my own path.

Carol and Colin

First day at School

Dancing Girl

Chapter 2

Instead of graduating into a good job, in July 1981, I started volunteering fulltime in a hostel for homeless women in Glasgow. The Broomielaw Hostel was run by the Glasgow Simon Community. It was home to nine women, if you could stretch your imagination to call it any sort of a home. A low concrete building, it sat on a bleak corner in a very rough part of the city, near the Anderson Bus Station. In fact, the hostel was a converted VD clinic which had cubicles rather than bedrooms, so the women could hear each other coughing and spluttering throughout the night. The hostel was 'dry', which meant that if anyone arrived back with a drink in them they were not allowed in, as the inevitable maudlin singing, swearing or crying then kept everyone awake. Us 'workers', as the volunteers were called, shared a small storeroom at the back of the building which housed one set of bunk beds and a chair. 'Workers' was an interesting job title as none of us were "workers" in the sense that we had ever seen the inside of a factory or worked a back shift. We were all young inexperienced students, idealistic and clueless. Three workers needed to be on duty at any one time which meant that two people got a bed and the third person slept on the floor. But we were very fair and had a rota for who slept in the bunk beds and who got the hard floor. Rotating beds also meant sharing the same sheets which worried me a great deal but it felt much too petty bourgeois to voice my concerns about preferring clean sheets every night. Instead, I recall using a sleeping bag under the sheets as a practical solution so that I could get a good night's sleep. The workers earned £7 pocket money a week for essentials and had two days off. Curiously, for a residential women's hostel, there was one male worker called Ninian who came during the day but stayed nights at the male hostel across the city. Of the nine women in the hostel, six were dead in half as many years.

Being in the hostel was hard. I was shocked out of my protective existence and my understanding of the world around me. The women's lives were dominated by alcohol, violence and prostitution. I watched the women leave the hostel in the morning knowing that the greater part of their day might be spent up a close by the bus station exchanging grimy sexual favours for a packet of fags and I wanted to be sick. I wanted sisterhood to mean that I could help these women and that they wanted my help. When they came back at night, it was hard to make eye contact, never mind revel in the sisterhood.

Still, the routine of running the hostel got us all through the day. One evening, I remember settling down with the women, after our dinner, in the small TV room which passed for a living room. The chairs were of the plastic wipe-down variety and the couch was more than second hand. That day, the atmosphere was fairly relaxed. Mugs of tea were being poured as the Coronation Street theme tune played in the background. Without warning, a brick was hurled through the window. It landed directly on the small coffee table between the chairs and the old couch, shattering mugs and spilling tea everywhere. The room was covered in glass.

This brick was the regular calling card of Hughie, long term 'man' friend of Hilda. Her 'man', as he was generally known, was also her pimp and if she refused to heed his request and go out on the streets, she knew what would happen. Hilda had a very ruddy complexion from drink, a flattened nose and no bone structure left to speak of, as Hughie had battered her face beyond all recognition up and down the pavement of the Broomielaw, alongside the river Clyde.

That night Hilda left and the rest of us cleared up the mess. The remainder of the evening was quiet, as the women exchanged knowing looks and we all dreaded Hilda's later return. If she had a drink in her, we wouldn't be able to let her back in, but how could she be forced to go up a Glasgow close or round the back of the bus station with a punter stone cold sober?

There were lighter moments too, with great warmth and humour. For me, fresh out of university, it was an entirely new kind of sisterhood. Despite it all, those women could tell a good story with lots of bad language and bravado about what they would do to their 'man' next time round.

'Bloody ejitt, he can go fuck himself if he thinks he can get round me wae two cans of Carlsberg, that'll be the fuckin day.'

'Ha, ha, damn right, hen, me tae.'

Hours could be whiled away over cups of tea with Hilda, Margaret or Cathy as they made light of their unhappy times with determined tales of survival and crude hilarity. All conversations were peppered with swearing and direct communication. *'Shut the fuck up,'* was how these Glasgow women asked someone to be quiet so they could hear the telly. The women also gave regular and unsolicited feedback on the cooking skills of the workers, which mostly revolved around who made the best scrambled eggs in the morning. I was regularly bottom of that list, *'Fuckin shite, hen, too runny an no enough salt.'* But they also had a soft spot for me because I was Scottish. I was one of them. The other volunteers came from far and wide with a somewhat romantic notion of helping the homeless in Glasgow. This was a kind of 'no mean city' precursor to your now fashionable gap year.

The Simon Community

21

Looking back, I felt welcomed into the bosom of a Scottish community that I really did not want to exist. It felt like the usual Scottish story of great people, feisty women, but shite times.

Cathy was short with dark hair and looked like me. She liked to show me pictures of her family. She cried a lot and then she drank some more. Mary was a short stout wee woman, almost as wide as she was tall, who had mild learning difficulties and had ended up on her own, homeless and living on the streets of Glasgow. She liked to help with the cooking and the endless peeling of potatoes. When I was new, she told me about the other women and their stories, about the Simon Community and all the different volunteers. Mary liked Ninian the best, as he had arranged weekends away from the hostel for the residents. I remember very well, one particular conversation with good natured Mary when unusually she lost her temper with me.

Mary: *'His mammy's got a palace you know.'*

Me: *'Really, Mary, is his mother's house nice?'*

Mary: *'Aye it's nice, 'cos it's a bloody palace.'*

Me: *'Do you mean it's really fancy? And big?'*

Mary: *'Naw hen, I mean it's a palace, his mammy's got a bloody palace.'*

Me: *'Ok Mary that sounds ... lovely, a lovely house ...'*

Mary: *'I'm tellin ye hen it's a bloody palace!'*

At this point, Mary slammed the tattie knife down hard on the kitchen table, pushed the chair back and left the room. I was left wondering what I had said to upset her so much when she came back into the kitchen a few minutes later clutching her favourite brown handbag under her arm. She opened her bag carefully and slowly took out some very dog eared photographs, telling me that this was the first time she went tae Ninian's hoose. She handed me her precious photographs.

There sat Mary, with a beaming smile at a long wooden table surrounded by suits of armour with Ninian sitting right beside her. Turns out that Ninian's other names are Lord Crichton Stuart, cousin to the Queen, owner of Falkland Palace and a founding member of the Glasgow Simon Community. Mary sat back down, looked at the expression on my face and smiled in triumph as she continued to peel the potatoes.

As we had to feed twelve people every day, the shopping list was enormous. We had to buy a mountain of bread and gallons of milk, not to mention the eggs to be scrambled and scored out of ten every morning. Shopping involved round trips to Henry Healey's, the local grocer along Argyle Street in the heart of the city centre. We had to shop in relays until someone discovered an old pram. Luckily it was the high up kind with big wheels. This made shopping much easier as we piled the pram with bread and milk and made our way through the city centre of Glasgow back to the hostel. One afternoon, on such a shopping trip, I bumped right into my mum and a group of her nurse friends who were all dressed in their finery out for lunch in the town. Mary turned to your Nana, unable to believe her eyes, '*Agnes, is that your Carol pushing a pram full of bread?*' Embarrassed and proud at the same time my mum said, *'Well, you know our Carol, since her weeest day, she does things her way, just graduated from uni too, but still, I suppose she is trying to help those less fortunate.'* They all gave me a couple of pounds to donate to the hostel and I trundled away with the pram piled high with the daily provisions.

On our days off, the hostel workers went to a flat provided by a supporter of the Simon Community on the south side, where the residential workers from the male and female hostels went to rest. It was there that another alternative community was forged, resulting a few years later in the sons and daughters of the Simon Community in a commune somewhere in Ireland. It was the eighties and being anti-establishment and political then involved second hand hippie clothes, josh sticks and being a militant vegetarian. Our days off in that flat revolved around

23

rolling fags and living off large pots of homemade soup. I never smoked, tobacco or anything else, and looked on from the margins wondering what it was all about. I remember a lot of committed folk in our early twenties, intense conversations about politics and lots of enthusiastic chopping of vegetables. While I had a shared commitment to doing good and enduring hardship, I was resisting a full blown transition to a hippie and still favoured high standards of personal hygiene. So, on my days off, I sometimes went home to Motherwell instead and took various unwashed friends with me for a proper hot bath and tinned tomato soup. Your Nana and Papa very generously welcomed an assortment of people into their home and kept the questions about when I would get a proper job to a minimum. Nana was a bit nervous about meeting vegetarians and practically bought up the health food shop in Hamilton. I remember that she sent John, the first of many friends I brought home, back to Glasgow with loads of Tupperware boxes full of soya and tofu.

After a couple of months at the hostel, I noticed that I was putting on weight. I put this down to large quantities of white bread. I struggled into my jeans and resolved to go on another diet soon. On one of my 'clean up' weekends, at home in Motherwell, Nana noticed my, by now, huge stomach. She worked nights in the hospital but also spent her days ever vigilant for the first sign of sickness or disorder, like a nurse/ policewoman famous for making secret doctors' appointments for reluctant patients. She marched me to the surgery.

I remember the Friday night after the GP appointment so well. The arrangement had been made to admit me to hospital first thing on Monday. I was consumed by anger and was *very* rude to our family visitors. Papa's only close family, his cousin Larry and his five sons, visited dutifully every Friday evening to play board games. They were very polite and conventional Catholic boys. In a foul mood I stated in no uncertain terms that no, I had not baked the cake that they were all enjoying with their tea, '*I have more important things to do with my life than*

24

bake bloody cakes,' and stormed off upstairs. As I slammed the door, I overheard my poor dad apologising for my behaviour as I had had bad news about "women's troubles" and had to go into hospital. They all ate their cake without another word while they laid out the Monopoly.

I had been told that afternoon that I had developed a huge cyst on my right ovary which had grown from the normal size of a thumbnail to the size of a football, twisting around and crushing other organs. I was admitted to hospital as arranged on Monday. They whipped it all out, and other bits too. I don't remember much about the operation itself, except that I liked the morphine, a lot.

I was most upset that it was my malfunctioning gynaecological anatomy that had landed me in hospital for emergency surgery. I wanted to have a more respectable medical disorder like a broken arm or leg. An ovarian cyst from the unspeakable and secret recesses of a woman's body, had a creepy sound, it was just plain embarrassing. Nana was mortified too that I was being so difficult, far from the ideal patient, in her hospital. Whether through her influence or the general consensus on the ward I was moved to a side room to rage on my own.

That first experience of being in hospital was awful. I was young, upset and bewildered. The busy routine of hospitals carried on around me taking very little account of my emotional distress or upset. So the operation was planned and I was drugged into silence as the pre-meds took effect. It was all very matter of fact. The next morning, before the operation, the indignities got worse as the flowery nightie was exchanged for the backless green hospital gown.

Nurse: *'Put this on please, and remove all jewellery except your wedding ring, you can keep that on and we will tape it around your finger.'*

Me: *'I am not married, I'm only twenty. I wear this*

silver feminist necklace though and I never take it off.'

Nurse: *'Well you will need to take off all jewellery, except your wedding ring, that's hospital policy.'*

Me: *'It can't do any harm, look its small and round my neck, it's not my neck that's the problem.'*

Nurse: *'There can't be any foreign objects, you are going under an anaesthetic and having an operation.'*

Me: *'But I want to keep it with me, for luck, can't you tape it down too?'*

Nurse: *'No it's against hospital policy.'*

Me: *'Well that's hardly fair is it? Why are wedding rings allowed then? If I take it off the chain it is quite small, see?'*

Nurse: *'The doctor will not be pleased but okay, let's see what we can do. There I'll tape it to your shoulder, that should be alright, okay now?'*

Me: *'Thanks, I'm a bit scared and hungry.'*

Nurse: *'Nil by mouth until the op is over I'm afraid, nothing to worry about, be over in no time and then you will be in the recovery room. As soon as you come round and come back to the ward we will get you some tea and toast. I've got to see to other patients now, but the porters will be along in a minute to wheel you to theatre.'*

When I came round from the operation, the nurse put the cup of tea and toast on the locker beside me, next to a small silver petrie dish holding a small silver feminist symbol.

Later that day, the doctor came to see me. I will call this first consultant Dr H. He told me that after the operation, I was left with half the necessary reproductive baby making equipment. He patted my feet and said not to worry, that I could probably still have babies. I was twenty years old, three

26

months out of university, making my own confused way in the world. I hadn't yet demonstrated that I could manage to look after myself, never mind another human being. I thought he was mad. At that stage, the thought of you hadn't entered my head. Not really. Not in any concrete way anyway, although my old next door neighbour Mrs Duncan swears that when I was eleven I told her in passing one day that *'When I grow up I am going to have lots of babies but I don't want a husband.'*

In hospital for two weeks, I was surrounded by mostly elderly women discussing their hysterectomies and prolapses. Jesus, it was awful. I had been in hospital only once before, when I was a child, to have my tonsils removed. This was very different. Then I had had time off school, I had felt special and had basked for days in the glorious attention of being a patient. I had loved the drama of being in hospital, the anticipation of the visiting hours, the presents and the comics. This time, no amount of flowers or cards made the situation any better. I was upset, embarrassed and above all angry. I sat up in bed one afternoon and wrote a letter to Spare Rib, the feminist magazine, about the unacceptable treatment of female patients in gynaecological wards in the NHS. Writing that letter, at least, made me feel a bit better. It was published and a few weeks later I received lots of letters from women who had similar terrible experiences. I had protested at least. *'Bastards,'* I thought, *'come near me again and I'll have the lot of you struck off.'*

While I was in hospital, I had an assortment of foreign visitors from the Simon Community who found their way from Glasgow to Wishaw, variously impressing and scaring members of our extended Lanarkshire family. My Nana, in particular - who up to this point had not been speaking to me for helping homeless women - *'An alcoholic woman is worse than a she devil'*- was very impressed when Ninian - *'The Queen's cousin you know, came to see our Carol'*- made a visit to Law Hospital. The others were generally regarded as unwashed hippies who should go and get themselves a proper

27

job. The week I was admitted to hospital, mum and dad had cancelled their planned holiday to Malta. They rebooked and took me with them to recuperate. Next thing, I found myself lying beside a pool keeping my scar covered, from belly button downwards, nothing small or discrete for me given my behaviour and the size of the cyst. I was in hospital for two weeks and then recovered for the next three before going back to work in the hostel and putting the whole miserable experience behind me.

How did it happen? They didn't know why or how ovarian cysts happen and couldn't tell me anything I could do to prevent it happening again. An unfortunate once in a lifetime miserable experience it seemed. I put it behind me and got on with my life. I did not go back for the six week checkup as I could not bear to see the inside of Law Hospital again. I went back to the hostel to continue with my mission of changing the world, or at least small parts of Glasgow.

Chapter 3

In 1983, after two years of voluntary work, I decided that I should go back to university to study Social Work. I was accepted for the Post Graduate Diploma in Social Work at Edinburgh University and worked in the Victoria Hostel for homeless women in Edinburgh at evenings and weekends to pay my way through university. At least, by that stage I had some experience of this 'work'. I had difficulty at first with the East Coast parlance in the hostel and could not distinguish the posh Edinburgh University lecturers from the true English, but other than that, I made a reasonably easy transition to living in Edinburgh. It was not quite as posh or unfriendly as the stereotypes had me believe. Although every time I opened my mouth, I was met with the response, *'Oh ... you're from the West.'*

As I was renting a room in a shared flat in Bruntsfield, I had to apply for Housing Benefit. During my first week at the start of October 1983, I recall walking up and down Princes Street like a tourist with map in hand, only I was looking for the Housing Department, not the castle. After a while, I stopped and asked a woman if she could direct me to the Housing Department on Waterloo Place. She was very helpful. *'Ken, ye cannae miss it, if ye walk right tae the very far end o' Princes Street ye will come to a big statue o' a man on a horse, pointing. Well, he is pointing ta the Housing Department on Waterloo Place.'* How very Edinburgh, I thought, Glasgow would just have put up a sign.

The Social Work course was divided into days at university and time on placements. My first meeting with my Director of Studies to discuss my areas of interest did not go well. He took one look at me sitting before him, with my short dark hair, my dungarees and feminist dangly earrings, telling him that I worked with homeless women and I wanted my first placement with Women's Aid. He decided that I needed to expand my horizons and perhaps he was right.

So instead of indulging my feminist crusade, my first placement was working with male adult offenders in the Pilton area of Edinburgh. I spent months writing reports on mostly unemployed young men involved in minor theft or Road Traffic Act offences. They either received fines or further probation orders which they ignored and as a result did further stints in either Polmont Young Offenders or Saughton Prison. This was in 1983 and the housing estates in Pilton and Muirhouse were very much then Irvine Welsh *Trainspotting* country. I remember going round the schemes doing home visits with my supervising social worker, Rob, who had long hair, wore John Lennon glasses and drove a cream 2CV. It felt like I had entered another strange new world.

The purpose of these placements was to ensure that students gained real experience of the world of social work clients. Having grown up in a council scheme myself, I could not work out what the hell I was supposed to do to help anyone, as we travelled around the streets in this 2CV. To me, the root causes of the problems all around were poverty and hopelessness. I was eager, but baffled. As part of my social work training, I had to take part in the duty rota in the Pilton social work office. This was grim stuff, every day of the week, with all sorts of people presenting themselves with all sorts of problems which really boiled down to not having enough money.

One afternoon when I was on duty, a mother of five children came in to the social work office with her kids complaining that her husband had received further fines. As usual, he had left her to sort it out. They were on benefits and she could not afford to pay his fines and feed the children. I asked her to wait and went off to my senior, Rob, to see how we could help. I was told in no uncertain terms that the state could not help her to pay court fines. I went back and explained very carefully to this woman that I could only help her if she had no money to feed her kids but not to pay fines. Quick on the uptake she went off and paid what she could that week to keep her man out of jail and then came back the very next day explaining that she was skint and needed money to feed her children. I was then able to fill out all the paperwork and give her a minimal amount of money to buy food for her five kids. Unfortunately for me, she then told all her friends and neighbours about the kindly young social worker from the west coast with the dark hair. It soon became obvious that when I was on duty the waiting room was full and the emergency cash payments were much higher. I was in big trouble and was told that it was not my job to give poor people money. But I thought that was the whole point.

The most difficult experience of my social work training happened during my second placement with a voluntary organisation in Edinburgh. They organised women's groups, helped single parents and sometimes offered counselling to young women with unplanned pregnancies. Somehow, even though still a social work student, I was assigned to the case of a nineteen year old woman who had become pregnant while working away from home. At first, she just wanted the chance to talk. She was a very intelligent young woman, quiet and dignified, even though her life was in turmoil. After the first few weeks, she decided to go ahead with the pregnancy and my role was to support her through it until she decided what she wanted to do. There was in depth discussion with the social work team about adoption and how the process worked, but I was also invited to her house to meet her parents who offered to support her and her baby. So this was very much her decision. Finally, in the end, when her baby boy was born, she decided to go through with adoption and I had to go to the hospital to collect the baby and take him to his temporary foster family.

I remember arriving on that maternity ward, ready to collect the baby. I had a taxi waiting. That day, like most days, the nurses had been really busy and so had not been able to get the baby ready. I was handed this tiny baby and a bundle of clothes

31

by a harassed nurse. I was petrified. I just stood there staring at the smallest, newest baby I had ever seen and was frozen to the spot. The nurses thought I was worse than useless. After a painful few minutes, one nurse came over and changed the baby quickly, handing him back to me with an understanding smile. I then had to walk out of that hospital with this small newborn baby in my arms and take him to foster parents. He stayed there for six weeks to allow his mum to visit in case she wanted to change her mind. I went on the bus with her every week to visit the baby but she did not waiver.

There was no shortage of families waiting to adopt a new born baby, so the adoption process was quick and relatively straight forward, for the social workers and adoptive parents at least. More time was again built in to allow for any change of heart but the adoption was finalised and the baby started his new life in his new home. This was the first of many cases of adoption which I will never forget. On the baby's first birthday, although I had moved on in my course, I remembered his mother's address and sent her a card just to let her know I was thinking about her. I got a lovely card back telling me that she had started college and that she had no regrets. Years later, I still think of that mother and baby and wonder how things worked out for them both.

For my last placement, I was finally sent to Women's Aid in East Lothian. I struggled to understand why so many women put up with cruel and degrading treatment from the very people who professed to love them. Women would most often finally leave to protect their children. The refuges were always full, as domestic violence happened every day of the week in every town and city in Scotland. I remember one woman being declared intentionally homeless. The male housing officer had visited her husband who flatly denied the abuse and reassured the council that it was perfectly safe for her and her kids to return to the family home. She had to remain in the refuge while further legal advice was taken and Women's Aid successfully fought her case to have the violent husband removed from the house.

In July 1985, I qualified as a social worker. My first job was with a temporary Welfare Rights team set up to challenge the Conservatives' removal of benefits to the young homeless. Many young people had gone to ground, naturally suspicious of our efforts to help them while another arm of the state had made them destitute in the first place. Thatcher years indeed, no compassion and certainly no joined up thinking about the needs of her non-existent society. Then it was very easy to know what you were against, and as a feminist it was tragic that we all hated the first ever female Prime Minister. Best summed up by my Nana. '*That bloody woman, she would take the eye oot yer heid and tell ye ye looked better withoot it.*'

When that six month temporary contract finished, I contemplated what to do next and by sheer chance saw an advert in New Society magazine for a social worker tutor needed to work with a child in Sudan. Before I knew it, I was in London for an interview at Great Ormond Street Hospital with the child's psychiatrist and her key worker, Simone Harty. So that is how I first met Simone who became an important friend and part of our lives. But that comes later.

Within a week, I got the job and was arranging to go to Sudan. When I phoned home and said where I was going, we all had to look at a map of Africa to find out where it was. I flew off to Khartoum in January 1986 to work with a thirteen year old girl with mental health problems. Strangely, I then found myself in the lap of luxury living with a wealthy Sudanese family full of doctors and lawyers who were struggling to come to terms with this different child. Looking back, I don't think I helped that girl very much. We tried to establish a routine and attempted some home tuition but she was very violent and I remember being regularly beaten up and trying to defend myself as she was well made and as tall as my own five foot three.

Of course, I had back up from the doctors in London by

phone and fax and we experimented with her medication levels. The doctors advised her family to get her to exercise to tire her out and to combat the weight gain which was a side effect of the drugs. They recommended jogging. We had to drive to a quieter part of Khartoum away from her immediate family and neighbours, let her out of the car and slowly drive along as she ran behind us. What seemed like a good idea to us then caused no end of commotion as lots of puzzled children ran after the car yelling at us to stop and pick her up thinking we had left her behind.

The doctors were reluctant to put a label of schizophrenia upon such a young girl. The family just tried to cope as best they could and all I could do was reassure them. The father was for some reason in political exile in Egypt. Above my bed was a large photograph of him shaking hands with Yasser Arafat. I thought it better not to ask too many questions about their family affairs, and steered very well clear of any political discussions. Because of the father's exile, the eldest boy was therefore head of the family. He was at university studying engineering and would come home late at night and wake his mother so that she could make him something to eat. She had very often had the day from hell but she dutifully got up and tended to this young man, who as I saw it, could easily have made his own supper. I remember having words with him about this, but my protestations fell on deaf ears. I only gained respect in his eyes when I managed to help him with his calculus homework. Fortunately for me, he had made a fairly simple but glaring error on the first page of his calculations and my rusty maths was good enough to pass him back several pages with the correct answer at the end. He was stunned into silence. This family was rich by anyone's standards, but they were also kind to me and were struggling with a very sick child. This experience was short lived, as the child had to be readmitted to hospital in London three months later. I've no idea what happened to her as we lost touch a few years later. I have a photograph of me with a goat tied to a tree. They had arranged a special dinner for me which was to involve slitting the throat of the goat and roasting it. I had to explain that I didn't think all the blood and guts would be a good idea and besides, I was a vegetarian. They all thought I was most unusual, especially as my mum had made me pack a raincoat, just in case. Blighted by drought for years, they hooted with laughter that the Scottish girl brought a rain coat to Sudan. Whenever we had visitors, I was always asked politely to go upstairs and come down wearing my reversible black and grey raincoat. Anyway, they accepted my vegetarianism and at least the goat survived to live another day.

When I returned to Scotland, I applied for a job as a social worker with Strathclyde Regional Council, then the biggest local authority in Scotland. I had to go through a panel interview and then could be allocated a job anywhere in the Region from Girvan to Oban. I ended up back in my home territory of Lanarkshire as a social worker in Bellshill. That's when I had my first red Mini. I used to drive around the schemes, doing home visits, feeling important that I had a purpose to help as many families and children as possible. At first, I loved being a social worker. I also loved that red Mini.

As a generic social worker in a local authority team, I was very quickly dealing with child abuse cases, as well as fostering or adoption. I decided to go back to university part-time to do a two year Certificate in Women's Studies. I started a part-time Masters degree at Stirling University. Working with families and child abuse was draining and a very thankless task. Social workers must have one of the most difficult jobs in the world, being responsible for keeping children safe, charged with the responsibility of doing risk assessments which require second sight and a crystal ball while the rest of the world turns a blind eye.

I also found myself becoming attached to some of the children. There were some very sad tales. One wee boy had been left alone in the house aged three. His dad was long gone

35

and his teenage mother had struggled to cope alone. One day she just moved on too, leaving this wee boy alone in the house, crying and hungry. We took him into care and had to find a foster placement for him. I would visit him every week while we tried to track down his family. I took him out for a treat once or twice a week, maybe to the park or to McDonald's and worked on a Life Story book for him as we made arrangements for his adoption. One day, I arrived in my red Mini to take him out and one of the other foster children shouted to him, '*Your mummy is here.*' He came running down the stairs with a huge smile of excitement on his face which was crushed when he saw it was only me, his social worker, not his mummy. He was the most gorgeous wee boy and it was absolutely heart breaking. I could have taken him home with me to adopt myself but it was almost unheard of in those days for single people to adopt. He was eventually settled in a lovely family in Glasgow. That wee boy must be nearly thirty by now and I hope that his adoption worked out well.

*

My next social work job involved working with a Women's Aid Group, which had acquired three year funding from the European Community to open refuges and provide an advice service for women and children experiencing domestic violence. I gave up my permanent Social Work post with the child abuse cases and the final salary pension to work collectively within a feminist voluntary organisation.

Chapter 4

During the Christmas holidays in 1988, I was on call covering the refuges. I had just delivered another load of Christmas toys to the kids and was looking forward to a New Year trip to meet up with friends in London. I was packed and ready to go the day after Boxing Day. By this time, I was renting a one bedroom flat from a housing association in Hamilton. It was small and, best of all, easy to clean. My enthusiasm for decorating my first flat led me to make bold choices; green and red apple wallpaper in the small kitchen and bright yellow and white vertical stripes in the bathroom. It looked nice and fresh in the shop, but I couldn't put on the light in the bathroom if I had a hangover. Otherwise, I was settled and happy in my flat and my job.

That night, I decided to go to bed early but couldn't sleep for a terrible pain which kept coming and going. I got up several times and took some painkillers but the pain just got worse. I couldn't see my GP due to the Christmas holidays, so I decided to be sensible and try to get medical help. I waited until the morning and phoned my friend Maxine who was also a social worker with Women's Aid. Although it was the Christmas holidays, she came round and drove me to the casualty department of Monklands Hospital.

We waited for a long time in hard plastic chairs in a deserted hospital, cheered up with a few bits of tinsel and a crooked, false, Christmas tree with a rather worn out looking fairy on top. Both had seen better days. Eventually, a young male doctor appeared and finally examined me. Given my previous unmet demands for a female doctor when I was in hospital the first time, I protested less and just wanted to be on my way. This doctor's attitude softened as he explained that he needed to find a consultant. Dr C then appeared looking concerned. After a bit more prodding and poking around (and questions about my previous scar and operation), I was taken to another department to have a scan. Before this, I had to consume vast quantities of water until I felt as though I might burst with discomfort. But I was told in no uncertain terms that I *must not burst* as, just before I can't possibly drink anymore, will be the ideal time for the scan. I was left sitting in a wheelchair in a hospital gown with a large jug of water and a glass.

Merry bloody Christmas.

After the scan, I was immediately admitted to hospital again with another outsized ovary. This second time they told me that it could be life threatening as it was so big it could burst or damage other organs. The consultant told me that I had no choice but to have another operation. Tragic certainly, he says shaking his head, with me so young, as no ovaries means no children, but such is life. These things happen. Even more tragic since it was Christmas, but there you are, could be worse. Papers are produced. Sign here please.

I asked Maxine to call my mum and my friends in London to tell them I wouldn't be coming. At first I refused to give my permission for another operation. It all seemed so final. I told the doctor that I was going to discharge myself to have time to think about things. '*No you are not,*' was his abrupt response. '*I will not allow it. You need to be sensible. You could die if it ruptures.*' I argued with him, and still wouldn't believe him so he brought me a large medical text book with bloody gynaecological abnormalities and dropped it on my bed. '*Read that,*' he said, leaving the consent forms beside me.

Meanwhile, the nurses were being harassed by numerous phone calls from my London alternative social work friends. They were trying to mount a long distance campaign against radical surgery, making lots of suggestions about alternative therapies; new age workshops and remedies in humming, massage, crystals, herbs, anything but surgery. Simone said she would fly up to Glasgow if I couldn't come down and she cancelled all of her New Year plans. The nurses thought that my friends were bonkers and I became the centre of attention on the quiet ward. During a handover at the start of another shift I heard one nurse say, '*Did you hear about all that fuss? All the phone calls? That young social worker lassie, has to have her other ovary out, she won't be able to have kids, she's that young too, shame. Christmas as well, shame, she is first on the list for tomorrow.*'

When all the fuss died down and the phone calls stopped, I locked myself in the toilet and I cried, lots. The nurses left me alone. For hours, I sat there on that toilet, cold and uncomfortable but determined not to go back to my hospital bed to inhabit the persona of a patient. I tried, with all my might, to will myself into another situation, to force the world beyond the toilet door to disappear so that when I emerged there would be no consultants, no concerned nurses, and no operating lists. I will not allow this to happen to me again, I told myself. I will put on my coat and I will walk away. I will show them.

But the doctor's dire warnings of serious consequences played on my mind. He refused to discharge me, so that I would need to leave against medical advice and be left wondering forever about the wobbly exploding mass in my abdomen. This didn't seem like an intelligent choice. Eventually, I grew resigned and accepted that I had no choice.

I spent the rest of that night in that toilet, thinking about never being a mother, about never having you. I thought about my own childhood and the problems your Nana had working and bringing up two children. My dad worked long days and she worked constant night shifts in the hospital, learning to power nap at will around school hours when the opportunity arose, surviving on very little sleep. She had had two children in quick succession and any problems with motherhood for her definitely revolved around me and my behaviour, rather than my big brother. My childhood was peppered with tales of my antics, even as a very young toddler I had to be strapped into the high chair out of harm's way or put in my cot and then I would stand up, rattling my empty bottle along the wooden

39

bars, shouting in a loud voice '*Agnes, milk,*' until she fulfilled my demands. She tells lots of stories. For example, that as a toddler I used to climb the fence over to the neighbours and shout through their letter box that it was time to get up and come out to play. My mum tells less amusing tales of being taken aside at Brownies and being told by Brown Owl that I was a disruptive influence, perhaps better suited to other activities. My mum's explanation for her unexpectedly strong-willed daughter, who resisted all attempts to be socialised into femininity, who was expelled from Brownies, asked to leave ballet lessons, talentless at piano and colloquially outspoken in spite of those expensive elocution lessons, lends more to the 'dropped on the head as a baby' theory than to genetics: '*Your brain went into spasm when you were born and it has never stopped rattling around your head ever since!*'. Nana repeats that like a mantra when I mention some new idea or plan. Of course, she may just be right.

Maybe, I thought that night, motherhood was to be one of these activities I just wasn't suited to, like dancing or collecting badges at the Brownies for good needlework. I wondered too, if I had been a good Catholic, would I have had good, well behaved ovaries? I wondered if I had been too clever for my own good? That night lots of questions like these kept going around and around in my head for hours. If I had been more content with my lot would I be in this predicament? Has being a feminist from a young age caused my ovaries to explode? The only answer appeared to be that whatever else I managed to achieve in life, I was not going to be a mother, never destined to meet you.

I cringed too, as I remembered one particular day when, aged eleven, I announced to the world that I *could* have a baby.

*

It is 1972, my last year of primary school. Our teacher, Miss Mullen, who is very strict with a very keen penchant for the belt, is off sick with a brain tumour. We have another temporary teacher, Mrs. McGowan. She is retired and must be around eighty, I think. She has a very deep scary voice and large floppy jowls. She is old fashioned and even stricter than Miss Mullen. I am watching my step, trying not to talk too much. Unfortunately, she already knows my granny through the chapel and tells me that she has heard all about me and she has me marked down as a troublemaker. I stay silent, but scowl. I had not even opened my mouth.

This ancient gruff teacher dispenses with lesson plans or any revision for the 11 plus exam. Instead, she sends the boys out of the class to do woodwork every single day, so that she can tell the girls about periods and having babies. A whole year of school is spent learning about menstruation, which is somewhat unusual in a Scottish Catholic primary school in 1971. We girls just love it, especially as an alternative to complicated sums and fractions. It becomes a competition in the class with the clever girls in the top group thinking up more and more obscure questions and references to internal body parts. I am best at it and I get braver by the day. Hand in the air and in my best loud voice, *'Please miss, what is a uterus?'*

A big hush descends with nudges and giggles before the boys are sent out of the class yet again to do more woodwork. The girls love it and the boys make lots of tables. However, these were still the days of selective education and the 11 plus exam. The other top class in the next room, are quietly working away, doing endless arithmetic revision and past papers. But then, they know very little about periods and have absolutely no clue what you can do with a uterus. Predictably enough, our class does not perform as expected in the 11 plus exam.

As far as I remember, our individual results were never announced. The headmaster, Mr. Sherry, merely wrote to all parents telling them that the whole class was being held back to repeat the year which would not be a problem as we were the younger top class, having started school in the January. We were all just eleven. No harm done. Even though it transpired

41

that a number of us had passed our 11 plus, all pupils were to be held back to repeat the school year.

Imagine the reaction of your aspiring *education is your passport to life* and *the only hope for our wayward daughter* grandparents, who saw my rattling hyperactive brain as my only saving grace. They went spare. Or, at least secretly spare. They vented their rage with the authorities and took on the establishment. But they didn't ask me.

Coincidentally, and somewhat ironically, that very same summer of 1972, age eleven, I started my period. I was, in the circumstances, very well prepared for this event following my year of immersion in menstruation (so to speak). You read all these accounts of menstruation of girls knowing nothing at all, thinking they were about to die a horrible death in the school toilet. Not me. I was excited. It seemed to me at least by then a perfectly natural and acceptable subject of polite daily conversation as I proudly announced to all friends, neighbours and even occasional visitors to the house that I could have a baby now if I wanted, as I knew all about periods and what to do with my uterus. Perhaps that was the same day as the no husband conversation with Mrs. Duncan, our next door neighbour? And it seems that forty odd years later, I have continued in the same vein, telling the world about my wayward ovaries.

During these same summer holidays in the early seventies, I became aware of furtive discussions. Mum was up during the day despite working night shifts and dad was home from work, both of them were over-dressed in suits and finery without going to any weddings or funerals. I asked questions about where they were going but was just fobbed off. It transpired that they were not going to take the decision of old Mr. Sherry, the headmaster, or the Lanarkshire Education Authority lying down. They had taken advice and had formally appealed against the decision to keep me at primary school for another year. This was unheard of in deepest Lanarkshire where parents respected and very much deferred to teachers.

The appeal of course unearthed the whole scandal of Mrs. McGowan and her year long period talks. The headmaster was forced to open the school during the summer holidays to let the education authorities review the records of all pupils in my class. Then something of a cover up was attempted between the headmaster and the local education authority, who thought they would see off one set of pushy parents as no other family had appealed. The appeal was turned down and I was to go back to primary school with all the class. My parents with blind faith and sheer determination took further legal advice and challenged the decision again, taking the appeal right up to the Secretary of State for Education in Scotland. They were angry as hell.

All this was going on behind my back and although, with the best of intentions, no one thought to ask me what I wanted. At that time, I was best friends with Ann Callaghan. She lived in the next street and we had made our best friend plans to move to America and become famous as soon as possible. She had an aunt there who was going to smooth our path and give us a place to stay. We had it all worked out. I first saw colour television at Anne's house when she invited me to watch Scooby Doo and have tea. The colour TV was amazing and we had fish fingers followed by a Birds Eye individual mousse, each. I thought they were very posh. I intended to stay best friends with Ann until we left Scotland for our better lives in America.

Two days before the start of the new term in August 1972, my parents received an official letter in a brown envelope all the way from Edinburgh saying that I could start high school after all. We then had to go emergency school uniform shopping and much to my surprise, and my friends', who were walking back to school wearing their brown uniforms to St Brendan's Primary School, I was on a bus in a navy blue blazer and school skirt on my way to Holy Cross High School

43

in Hamilton, six miles away. That day I wasn't at all sure about the potential of my reportedly clever brain or the future possibilities of my uterus.

*

Sitting alone in that hospital toilet so many years later, I was amused by the certainty and brashness of my younger self. But I realise with an empty thud that there are no future possibilities of my uterus. I felt faint and tired from all the crying and my head hurt from too much thinking and lack of sleep. My thoughts were muddled and I felt like I was falling down a large black hole, yet I was desperate to keep a grip and to feel the concrete edges and challenging possibilities of my future life. Perhaps, I thought, if you are clever and a feminist, you are not meant to have babies? Perhaps this is a message from God to become a Catholic again and start going back to mass? Well, then again, perhaps not. Maybe I thought it is a cosmic sign that I need to concentrate on my brain and my career. Not so much 'nature versus nurture' that I wrote essays about on the social work course. More nature versus neurons, brains versus babies, career versus motherhood. Perhaps I am not meant to be a mother, I thought that night, because I was going to do something extraordinary and spectacular with the rest of my life. Maybe if I don't have children, I thought, I would go and live in America after all, where I would achieve great things. I spent all night trying to convince myself that what was happening made sense, that I would be courageous and tragic at the same time. That I would overcome, somehow. That night I said a very tearful goodbye to you and tried to think of another kind of future without motherhood.

In the morning, I was exhausted but calm. I was resigned. I emerged from the toilet and I signed the forms. No ovaries. No kids. Oh well, I wanted to change the world anyway. I told myself that I would lead a noble and political life after all. But I wasn't convinced.

The atmosphere was heavy as I was prepared for the second

operation and given my pre-meds. The only thing I looked forward to was the morphine. No one knew what to say. I could tell that my mum was upset too. She was fussing around the room organising lots of vases of flowers. She had once again bought me new matching sets of dressing gowns and night dresses making sure that I had everything I needed, so that I would be the star patient in the ward, above and beyond any criticism from the nurses or other patients. I watched her in silence as she organised my locker. I imagined that she was thinking too about the grandchildren she would never meet. But she tried her best to be reassuring. She knew I was devastated, as I was so quiet and had stopped complaining or asking questions. Then she stopped fussing around the room and sat down beside me. She always tried to look on the bright side. My mum took my hand and said, '*Never mind darling, it could have been a drug addict or a terrorist or anything.*'

I was completely lost for words as the drugs kicked in.

GYNAECOLOGICAL SURGERY

INFORMATION FOR PATIENTS

Cover of information leaflet provided to patients.

Chapter 5

When I came round from this second operation, I was still groggy and in pain. There was a drip in my left hand and I couldn't move without great discomfort. The nurse saw that I was awake and soon the therapeutic, post operative, tea and toast arrived. She helped to lift me up the bed a little so that I could reach it. Then she went to fetch the doctor.

Dr C then approached in his white coat. Smiling. *'Some bedside manner,'* I thought to myself, *'what the hell is there to smile about?'*

He sat down beside me. Through the haze of morphine, I heard strange words.

Dr C: *'Same ovary, happened again, took it out properly this time. Unusual to regrow like that, and another cyst, very unusual ... very strange, never seen that before, but not to worry. It's good news for you ... you have one ovary left. You might be able to have children after all.'*

I was silent and very puzzled.

I think I must be dreaming. Concentrating on my tea and toast, I am not at all sure what he is saying to me but I am tired and don't ask many questions. I am not encouraged to ask questions. It has all worked out for the best it seems. He patted my feet. Then he moved on to see the next patient while I finished my tea.

When discharged from hospital in January 1989, just as I am turning twenty-eight, I weighed seven stone and ten pounds. Two operations later I miraculously appeared to still have one functioning ovary. Either I am the bionic woman wantonly re-growing malfunctioning reproductive organs or medical science does not have all the answers.

I don't ask any more questions. Instead, I resolved to become a mother while I could, I wanted to have you before it is too late.

Discharged from hospital I was the skinniest I had ever been as an adult, but alas, there are no photographs of my skinny self, as my birthday dinner was recorded with smiling, happy people clicking away with no bloody spool in the camera.

Very soon after this second operation, I knew that waiting to have a baby some vague time in the future with a good-looking, intelligent, brown-eyed, Marxist was much too much of a gamble. Besides which, they seemed few and far between in the West of Scotland and sadly even in London. During my teenage years, I had been caught up in class wars and gender wars and had little interest in romance. Maybe it was my dodgy ovaries and hormones but I had a very different perspective on life. When I saw my friends at university, intelligent young women, getting dressed up in their gypsy skirts and blue eye shadow to go out 'on the pull' around the pubs of Glasgow, I wondered what the hell they were up to. It seemed to me a wholly pointless and demeaning experience. After the first few times, I left them to it and preferred to stay home with my intellect, thinking of higher things. My take on women's liberation was to respect oneself and be utterly discerning, not to be flattered by the passing attentions of inferior creatures besotted by football and drinking. By my late twenties, I had softened this stance somewhat and had encountered a few would be Marxists. But I was still discerning and single.

I bought and read dozens of books and established a small library debating the pros and cons of motherhood. Although I was dealing with the shock of the second operation, I was not lost in some dewy-eyed broody, maternal instinct. Far from it. I bought lots of angry feminist tomes like *Mad to be a Mother* and other litanies on the evils and oppression of motherhood, how it robs a woman of her career, her looks, costs a fortune and ultimately the cute babies grow up into ungrateful adults blaming all their ills on their poor mothers. I tried very hard to dissuade myself. But nothing worked.

There I was, a feminist desperate for a baby – a constituency

47

of one. Being a militant feminist desperate for a baby was a secret which I nursed and protected until I felt able to voice the words out loud: '*I want a baby.*' I knew it was unusual to be a feminist desperate for a child but I had such a strong gut feeling that it was right for me and, if it was possible to have a child before my remaining ovary exploded, then I would be the very best mother I could be.

Around the same time, I was very much aware of the reality and risks of pregnancy and true life tragedy. My younger cousin, the second grand-daughter of my generation, had given birth to the first great-grandchild of the next. Tragically, the baby was born profoundly disabled, as part of her brain had not formed during pregnancy. Again, doctors could find no reason, no genetic explanation, no fault, just a tragic, profoundly unlucky and devastating accident of birth, leaving an otherwise beautiful baby girl unable to see, hear, speak or with the ability to get to know her heartbroken family. This was sad beyond belief for my cousin and her husband and for the first few months they were in shock. She looked just like any beautiful baby girl, dressed to perfection in lovely dresses and matching bootees. My mum often looked after the baby to give my cousin a break and one day when I was visiting there she was lying on the sofa fast asleep. It was so hard to accept that anything was wrong with such a small scrap of humanity. Mum asked me to watch her while she went out to hang out some washing. She had very strict rules of etiquette for hanging out washing so that the neighbours would see that she lived an ordered and respectable life – all sheets and pillow cases together, then towels, then shirts, then trousers, before the smaller items of pants and socks. If I failed to hang up the washing in strict rotational order she would go out and peg it all up again muttering under her breath but loud enough to hear, '*If you want things done properly, do it yourself.*' while I would mutter right back that the washing dried despite the way it was hung up. That is not the point, I was told. I still don't get that point.

That day, no sooner had my mum started to hang up the washing in her proper order than the baby woke up and started to have a seizure right before my eyes. I was petrified and shouted for mum to come quick. She came in and with her years of nursing experience tended to the baby, administering medicine and making sure she was safe while the seizure eased. Meanwhile I watched with such a feeling of sadness and helplessness, proud of my mum, yet too scared to pick up this small human being to cuddle and comfort her, in case I did her more harm than good.

This reality completely dispelled any fantasy notions of talcum-powdered babygros with little feet and cuddly toys. I was only too aware of the reality of what can and does go wrong in life and especially in pregnancy. I thought very long and hard about, if or how, I could cope with a disabled child. I wasn't sure that I could. I wanted a healthy baby, I was not in the least bothered about whether I might have a boy or girl, but I prayed that my baby would be healthy.

Despite the fear that this family tragedy instilled in me, I could not rid my head of thoughts of babies. It was contrary and I knew it. I was single. I was scared. I was a bolshie feminist, a determined and independent woman. Yet more than anything, I wanted a baby. No matter how many books and horror stories I made myself read, I could not be dissuaded. The stark choice of living life with or without a child was uppermost in my mind, every minute of every day, no matter how busy I tried to be, throwing myself back into work and Labour Party politics. I had remained politically active since university and spent nearly every evening out at one Labour Party meeting or another. I was frequently referred to as the wee lassie at the back of the room as I tried to raise objections or understand what the hell was going on. I volunteered to be the Constituency Womens' Officer and then got into hot water by advertising the Women's Sections meeting in the local paper. It seemed that one of the women had arranged with her husband that we could meet in a room in the Railwayman's

Club in Hamilton, free of charge, as long as we kept it secret and didn't cause a commotion. So the same group of six or seven women met in this secret back room, brought scones, organised raffles and fundraisers and failed to discuss all women shortlists or any politics of any substance whatsoever. Try being a militant feminist in that environment, it was demoralising and exhausting.

In the eighties, the debate was not about women having it all. In my day you had to sign up early, for which bit of 'it' you were prepared to settle for, then life for women was a straight choice, one or the other but most definitely not both, not a career *and* motherhood. Oh, no. When I was at high school, one teacher, exasperated with my daily litany of the feminist struggle, the oppression of womankind and how I was single-handedly going to change the world, lost the plot and screamed at me with unconcealed venom that I was no different from the rest, that she would meet me down the launderette with my eight weans just like everyone else and the sooner I got used to the idea the better! So from a young age, girls of my background were taught not to expect much and brainwashed to believe that whatever did come our way was beyond our control and involved lots of babies and little money. Ambitious women of my generation have fought against this kind of brainwashing determined to make our mark, to go to university and have a successful career, unencumbered by the eight weans. So by the eighties, there was a well-trodden path towards motherhood and a new exit route for women with shoulder pads which pointed to a career, but there was no intersection or map to tell you how you could reach both. For those of us on the new route to a profession, there was no road which allowed you to double back and pick up children. Then, career and motherhood were two parallel but entirely separate roads.

In some ways, there was less pressure than today because we were expected to align ourselves with one or the other fairly early on. Nowadays, young women like you are expected to

50

be clever and studious, yet also attractive and attentive to boys all at the same time. Even after fifty years of the second wave feminism of the sixties, there seems to be less leeway to reject that social conditioning of being a size zero in favour of brains. At least in my day, we could reject one stereotype while embracing the other, it was very much career woman versus motherhood, but never both.

Back then, before I broached the subject of babies with close family and friends, I started to do some research. This was the age of scary AIDS adverts with large gravestones and dire warnings, so meaningless, unprotected sex to become pregnant did not seem, to me at least, to be a sensible or ethical option. Besides, this was my decision.

In March 1989, I went back for my follow-up appointment to the hospital to see Dr. C. I was given the all clear and told that the half measures I had left were in working order. Nevertheless, I felt that I had no time to waste before my only remaining ovary malfunctioned. When I was told all was physically okay following my check-up, I started to think very seriously and do lots of research contacting clinics in London. I wrote to the British Pregnancy Advisory Service in April 1989 and fully explained my predicament, my exploding ovaries and my desire to have a child before it was too late. There was an exchange of letters and phone calls to clinics in London and advice that I should get back in touch with my consultant gynaecologist so that he could make a referral for fertility treatment.

Considering what I had already been through, with the sympathy of the doctors before the operation (*so sad not to be able to have children and so young too, there, there*), I expected at least an understanding hearing. I made another appointment with Dr C at his clinic in Monklands Hospital. I felt confident that I could rationally and intelligently explain my considered thinking, my research and careful deliberations and ask for medical help to become a mother and have a baby

51

while I still could. That was the plan.

My stomach was churning as I sat in the waiting room. I was early but the clinic had started late. I was trying my best to avoid eye contact with the other women. I didn't want to compare disorders again. I had had enough of that in hospital. I should have brought a book, I thought, as I flicked through the women's magazines full of recipes and fashion choices. I timed the other patients as they went in and out of the doctor's room. It looked like each appointment lasted less than ten minutes so I will have to talk fast I thought, but not too fast, after all I want him to know I have thought about this and read lots of books. I needed to impress him, and be intelligent, thoughtful, professional, social worker, not so much of the stroppy feminist. Play it cool, I told myself, it will be fine.

Finally, my turn came.

> Dr C: *'Good afternoon, please take a seat. According to your notes you've had your six week post op check already? Any further problems?'*
>
> Me: *'No, not really, I am feeling much better.'*
>
> Dr C: *'So how can I help you today?'*
>
> Me: *'Well since I got out of hospital I have been doing quite a lot of thinking.'*
>
> Dr C: *'Thinking? No need for that, just get better and put it behind you, though it might be a good idea to keep track of your monthly cycle from now on.'*
>
> Me: *'Yes, I've been doing that, trying to be healthy too. You said before when I was in hospital that doctors don't know what causes ovarian cysts in the first place.'*
>
> Dr C: *'No I'm afraid not, your case was unusual too, at your age in your twenties, two cysts on the same ovary is very unusual but nothing to worry about, really, don't worry, I've taken it all away this time, no need to worry.'*

Me: *'If there is nothing to worry about, can you tell me that it won't happen again to my good ovary, or what I need to do to prevent it happening to me again a third time?'*

Dr C: *'Well no, but you must not dwell on these things, too much thinking is not good for you, my dear.'*

Me: *'Actually, I've not just been thinking, I've been doing lots of reading too and I've been in touch with some clinics in London. After lots of thought I've made an important decision, I want to have a baby while I can and I need you to help me.'*

Dr C: *'Pardon? I don't understand what you mean.'*

Me: *'I want to have a baby while I can.'*

Dr C: *'But according to your notes you're not married?'*

Me: *'No, I'm single, but I am absolutely sure I want to have a baby while I still can.'*

Dr C: *'Oh no, no, no ... I don't understand at all, in exactly what way do you think I can assist you?'*

Me: *'Well, I've been in touch with some fertility clinics in London and they just need a letter of referral from you as my consultant telling them about my previous operations.'*

Dr C: *'Hold on a second, my dear, wait just a minute; are you seriously proposing to try to get yourself pregnant deliberately at a fertility clinic, out of wedlock?'*

Me: *'Well yes, lots of people have babies without being married these days and I want to have a baby while I still have the possibility, since I only have one ovary and you can't tell me when that might go wrong then I don't think I have time to wait or waste ...'*

Dr C: *'Now look, listen to me for just a minute, you are a very attractive young woman, stop all this thinking of* yours. *You've had an upsetting time, being in hospital. I remember you did not want the operation at all. It all went well. You are just upset. I am sure you will meet someone, fall in love, get married and have lots of babies, your Prince Charming might just be around the corner you know ...'*

Me: *'Well he might, or he might not, and even if he is, he might have fertility problems too. I am not upset, I am very sure. After what I've been through, twice now, I am just not prepared to take that chance of never being able to have a child. I want to have a baby by myself, my decision, my responsibility. I don't want to trick anyone into it and I don't want a reluctant partner, not fully committed to being a parent. I want to have a baby while I can. The clinics in London said all they needed was a letter of referral.'*

Dr C: *'This is NOT London. I can assure you that I am not in the habit of referring single young women to clinics to get themselves pregnant out of wedlock. I have never heard anything like this before in my entire career. These things might happen in London, but they most certainly do not happen here in Scotland. Not only will I not help you with this outrageous plan of yours, I will make sure that no one else in Scotland will give you the time of day. I beseech you to think again.'*

Me: *'But it is my body and my decision ... and I don't need to think again.'*

Dr C: *'Well in that case I cannot help you, if you don't mind I have other patients to see this afternoon. The nurse will see you out.'*

At least she smiled a little more sympathetically as she showed me the door.

Following this appointment, I received a follow up letter from Dr C beseeching me in writing not to have a child 'out of wedlock'. It was only many years later that I found out that Dr. C was a happily married father of seven. If I had listened to him, you would have remained but only a dream. That doctor had the power to change my life. I remember the outrage I felt the day I received his letter, still smarting from being unceremoniously thrown out of his clinic, facing a life of childless misery. What was so shocking after all about a woman wanting a baby? I was not about to be told no, least of all by him. If I had a chance of motherhood, then I wanted at least the opportunity to roll the dice and see what happened. But I had absolutely no idea where to start. The door had been so firmly slammed in my face.

I needed to be prepared before I went chapping on any other doors.

Chapter 6

Following this letter I was more determined than ever. 'Out of wedlock', indeed! What century was he living in, I wondered? In contrast, the response of the clinics in London was open and completely non-judgmental. They had no issue at all about treating single women, but wanted to know more about my medical history and gynaecological problems. I was still living and working in Hamilton, making determined enquiries to clinics in London which had no Scottish-style outrage and astonishment that a single woman wanted to have a child. This took many months of phone calls, letters, referrals to GPs, tracking down medical records, tracking my menstrual cycle, and finally, in October 1989, I received the much longed for letter from the British Pregnancy Advisory Service.

I opened it with such excitement, but it was worse than getting disappointing exam results. They said they could not offer me fertility treatment. Not because I was single, not at all. If I had been single but with two functioning ovaries I would have been on the next train south. Due to my 'complicated gynaecological history', they explained, they could not risk giving me fertility drugs or risk treatment without greater medical backup which was not available in their clinic. They could not manage my case, and with regret and great sympathy referred me to more specialised private fertility clinics. Back to square one. More letter writing.

In January 1990, over a year after my second operation, I arranged to go to London to see another doctor. Let's just call this one Dr G, at the Infertility Advisory Centre in London. He knew my medical history. He knew I was single. He arranged a consultation in London at a fee of £500 per hour. As I was working, I had scraped together the money and excitedly made plans to get to London. Fortunately I could stay with Simone, my social work friend, who had a spare room in her flat in Hackney. So off I went, excited, apprehensive, but very hopeful that after a year of letter writing, finally, someone was prepared to help me. The consulting rooms were just off Oxford Street, not quite Harley Street, but not far off. Suited and booted, I was prepared to make a good first impression, emphasising the thought and consideration that had gone into the past year since the second operation. By now, my image had softened somewhat. No longer the caricature feminist, I had gone underground and I could fool most people most of the time, well at least until I opened my mouth. I was determined to play it cool, if only I could quell my nerves.

Dr. G was friendly, helpful even. He listened to me very patiently. He took down all the facts of my two operations, clarifying what bits I had left, and whether they were functioning to the best of my knowledge. He then asked my age. I was healthy and I had cut out alcohol completely, was exercising regularly and taking the advice of the baby books, spending money on folic acid and multivitamins. I had just turned twenty-nine and I was a size ten. Ideal, I thought. I looked the picture of healthy, smiling womanhood as I sat in front of this next doctor.

Problem was, he said, that at just twenty-nine, he was not at all sure that I knew my own mind. I was, after all, a very attractive young woman, there might yet be time to meet Mr. Right. As politely as I could, I reminded him of the exploding ovary situation which had happened twice and that, at twenty-nine, I could naturally be the mother of a whole brood of children. Not to mention the fact that, as a qualified social worker, I had a responsible job, often making professional assessments and decisions about the welfare of other people's children. My cool resolve evaporated and my blood boiled. I told him that I was no wee lassie and I was not prepared to be patronised, especially as he had my full medical records and was fully aware of my age before the consultation and dragging me all the way down from Scotland to London. What exactly was his game?

Well, yes, he said he understood all of that, and while he had the greatest sympathy and respected my determination, he could not accept me for treatment at *only* twenty-nine. If I had been thirty-nine like most of his patients, he would not have hesitated. Or if, smiling at me, I had no other options (unsaid: if I was so plug-ugly I was unlikely to attract a man), then it might be another story. Or, even if the consultation had been arranged for another day and I had been seen by his female colleague, well that might have been different too. But, all in all, he was not happy to offer me treatment given my relatively young age. In his view I was just too young to know my own mind. While he meandered through all these different possibilities of me being a decade older, a different doctor, a different day of the week even, all I could hear once more was another senseless value judgment which could have a profound impact upon my life.

Once again I was outraged and dumbstruck by his callous, judgmental and frankly cruel charade of dragging me five hundred miles from Scotland to London, only to tell me he would not help me. Again, what I was hearing was far from a medical assessment. Sensing my fury he generously, or perhaps wisely, said in the circumstances, he would waive his fee for the consultation. Pay him? I wanted to kill him.

Again, I found myself out in the street, this time in London, with another door firmly slammed in my face with a man in a white coat behind it, holding it closed. His staggering hypocrisy rang in my ears. I could not fathom him telling me I was too young when all medical advice to women warned, alarmingly, of the tick/tock of the biological clock. I was blinded by tears of rage and frustration as I walked round the corner to Oxford Street. I remember standing at the bus stop, choking back tears, thinking, '*Where on earth do I go from here?*'

Once I was over the emotion and disappointment, each rejection just made me even more determined. I felt lost, always falling between two stools. The progressive clinics which treated single women would not take me due to my "complicated gynaecological history" and associated risks. Yet, the private fertility clinics in London which treated respectable couples (and perhaps *very* occasionally the odd desperate, very aged and plug-ugly single woman) would not accept me, because I was single and just too young to be in charge of my own destiny. I kept going from pillar to post, getting absolutely nowhere fast. At times it did feel hopeless but inside my head there was a voice telling me to keep going, not to give up and I had such a strong gut instinct and conviction that it was my choice. As a student, I had been on demonstrations for abortion rights when we would chant, '*Not the church and not the state, women shall decide their fate.*' I wanted to make the opposite choice to take control of my fertility to *have* a child. The same principles applied as far as I was concerned. It made me mad as hell that these paid up members of the patriarchy were telling me how to live my life and when I could have a child. So the feminist in me was furious and outraged, moved to tears of anger and frustration. '*How fucking dare they? Who the hell do these doctors think they are?*' As far as I was concerned, they were just grown up spotty boys who had been good at physics at school, had studied medicine because they were clever and now for some reason society handed them the divine power to decide on life or death. Not on *your* life and certainly not on mine. If I had the chance to become a mother at all then I wanted to do everything I could while I remained young and healthy, with one remaining ovary.

So the feminist debates would rage in my head, keeping me awake at night, but despite these intellectual pros and cons, when I woke up each morning my first conscious thoughts were about wanting a baby. I had to take deep breaths to get myself through the day and function as the determined feminist I projected to the world.

When I returned home from London and had gathered all my strength, I decided to retrace my steps and contacted

BPAS once again. I had nothing to lose. Rather than deal with things by letter or over the phone, I arranged to meet with their fertility specialist based in Brighton. I arranged time off and went to London again, then went down to Brighton by train. It was a long journey by train from Glasgow to London then on to Brighton, the equivalent of my pilgrimage to a new land offering new hope. Despite everyone else's doubts, I had to remain positive and focused on what might be possible. This time I met with a female specialist fertility nurse. She explained their concerns, that they would not be willing to use any powerful drugs or hormones. I gave her full reassurances that if I was finally accepted for treatment, this would be entirely at my own risk. Apart from the problem of plotting the activity of my one remaining ovary and my menstrual cycle, she was very concerned about the added problem of having fertility treatment in Brighton while living in Scotland.

No problem, I said, I would move to London.

And so finally, after so much rejection and disappointment I was accepted to start treatment at the British Pregnancy Advisory Service (BPAS) in Brighton in May 1990. This fertility journey was about to take me from Scotland to the very South of England.

Chapter 7

I immediately arranged six months unpaid leave from my job with Women's Aid. Fortunately, I could stay in Simone's spare room in her flat in Hackney. I asked my friend Linda to move into my flat in Hamilton. I also had to have a serious conversation with my mum and dad. At first they were very apprehensive and concerned. Your Papa, especially, echoed some of the doubts of the doctors. He could not understand this determination to have a baby. *'But I thought you were a feminist and a career women? Why do you want a baby? Children can bring a lot of heart ache and responsibility you know, are you sure you know what you are doing?'* Although they worried about the potential for disappointment, they reassured me that, as ever, they would provide whatever practical and financial support was necessary, as I prepared to turn my life upside down. I gave up my job and my home for six months and I headed to London.

At last, it was all systems go for me to start my first cycle of treatment in Brighton. I had been doing my Masters Degree, studying part-time at Stirling University, while working for Women's Aid. I arranged to finish my dissertation for my M.Sc. while in London.

Ironically, while I had been travelling up and down from London to Scotland, doing a Cook's tour of fertility clinics, accidental pregnancy was visited upon Simone. Just as she was about to embark on a six week tour of India her little blue line appeared. Simone had to consider serious and difficult choices as a single woman pregnant by an ambivalent and reluctant father. She decided to keep the baby *and* go to India. Although she was going through a traumatic time herself she was a great support and we lived through some strange experiences. I remember when Simone came with me to an appointment at the BPAS clinic. There we were sitting in the waiting room, Simone heavily pregnant about to have her baby, me hoping to have a baby someday, seated beside other women in the early stages of pregnancy seeking a termination. That waiting room represented the messy and complicated reality of women's lives and the challenges of controlling the means of reproduction. But that lived experience of women is never heard in these debates, so usually dominated by bishops and politicians who should show a great deal more humility and much greater respect for women. I can never understand how it is possible for politicians to have a free vote on abortion, while women seeking an abortion have no freedom to decide their fate. One abortion rights slogan sums it up nicely, *No womb, no say,* but in real life it is sadly not as simple as that. The waiting room at BPAS that day summed up those tensions and we were relieved to get back on the train to London.

Elliott was born on 15th April 1990, just weeks before I moved to London. Here I was, desperate for a baby of my own, sharing a flat with another single mother, and her beautiful baby boy. He was adorable with dark hair and big eyes.

Baby Elliott

I helped as much as I could, doing lots of practical things like cleaning the flat and keeping on top of endless washing, like a somewhat elderly Scottish au pair. Being around baby Elliott convinced me all the more that I wanted to have a child and it gave me a helpful apprenticeship and insight into the demands of young babies.

It was the hardest time in the world for Simone. She had hoped that Elliott's dad would see sense when the baby was born and either they would get back together or he would be part of Elliott's life, but this did not happen, despite me hand delivering letters and baby pictures on my frequent trips to Brighton where he lived. The first time I saw him was at Highbury Court, when he was refusing to pay any money for his son and the court seemed more interested in who the Scottish flat mate was and what she contributed to the household than ordering him to pay for his child's upkeep. It was horrible. Around that time I remember one trip to Safeway for food shopping. Unlike me, Simone was a good cook. She bought healthy food to cook from scratch, always watching the prices and what was on special offer. She educated me in the basics of cooking which I had rebelled against at school. It came as a huge surprise to me that cheese sauce did not have to come from a packet. Even though we had been careful, buying from a list, as we loaded up the food shopping at the till and the cash register bleeped its way through the weekly essentials Simone would be racked with anxiety. That day at Safeway she burst into tears as she realised how little she had left to live on for the week. All I could do was reassure her that everything would be okay but money, or the lack of it, was a constant source of anxiety.

Your grandparents were the first to voice their concerns that in the circumstances this move to London and sharing a flat with Simone and her baby was a recipe for disaster. What if I bonded too closely with Elliott and yet could not finally have a child of my own? That danger was there and I certainly grew to love that wee boy, almost as if he was my own. I remember

63

lots of happy hours at Clissold Park, the Early Learning Centre and Soft Play. Simone had her struggles, especially when she returned to work as a part-time social worker at the children's hospital in Hackney and then had to pay for childcare on top of everything else. It was an intense time and we tried to support each other with the unpredictable ups and downs of life. For me, living in Hackney was also very different from Scotland, but I grew to enjoy the trendy corner of London around Islington and Stoke Newington. Even though I had very little money either, I was happy to be of some help to my friend and ecstatic to be in London ready and impatient to get pregnant myself.

Elliott

Chapter 8

After plotting my cycle and checking dates, the first treatment at BPAS in Brighton finally arrived. I was dressed for the occasion as though I was attending the most important interview of my life. I made my way from Hackney to London Victoria to get the train. I was excited and confident. Sitting on the tube, I remember the adrenaline pumping. I was going to get pregnant and have a baby, soon. As agreed with the clinic, this treatment was low key drug free AID. I had been checking my ovulation by buying endless prediction kits from Boots and when it showed a surge in hormones, I had contacted the clinic. Timing the treatment within a forty-eight hour period was crucial, but it was no more scientific that that, a blast from a syringe, then a lie down for half an hour praying that I was making you. I was fit and healthy. I felt sure all would be well and, after all I had been through it felt as though you were meant to be. Following that first cycle of fertility treatment which was quite straight forward, I had to wait two weeks to find out if I was pregnant. I kept myself busy and tried my best to keep my mind on other things. When the day finally came, I unwrapped the pregnancy testing kit with a sense of jubilation and excitement. This was it.

Alas, no blue line. No pink dot. No pregnancy. I would not allow myself to cry. I kept being sensible. It was very early days, after all. *'Who gets pregnant first time anyway?'* I kept telling myself, *'I am in London now and I will make this happen.'* The next month brought the second attempt and trips to Brighton. Despite remaining upbeat, this was also negative. *'Shit. Damn.'* With a huge lump in my throat I told myself, *'Don't get mad, don't get upset, remember the importance of karma, be positive, talk nicely to your only ovary, it is only a matter of time. Relax. This is meant to be.'* Third time lucky, perhaps?

Nope. In July 1990, there was still no pregnancy and my

brave face was beginning to slip. It was half time, half way through my six month sabbatical in London and still nothing doing. *'Breathe. Fuck. Breathe'*. Between cycles and helping Simone with Elliott, I was travelling to the Women's library in Aldgate, East London to finish my dissertation for my M.Sc. At least, this gave me another focus. The library was then housed in a basement and I spent long hours underground reading feminist books about how the personal was political. *'Damn right,'* I thought.

During the next cycle in August 1990, I was called in to see the clinic nurse. A routine test had detected another possible problem: abnormal cells. I got a very frank talking to from a no-nonsense nurse who recommended further investigations. No point she says in having a baby only to die of cancer before it is five years old. Well, quite. I had to agree even if the message was delivered with all the sensitivity of a very cold speculum. So I agreed to delay and have more tests. I then found myself on the rocky shingle beach in Brighton looking out to sea and feeling utterly desolate. There were times when you seemed so elusive, beyond my reach, although I always looked after you in my imagination.

I called home to speak your to Nana, as my mum but also as a nurse. She told me that day that she had been given a drug when she was pregnant with me called DES. When I got back to London, I did some research on this drug and called a support group in Canada. This drug, full name Diethylstilbestrol, has been linked to fertility problems in the next generation, known as DES daughters. At last, a possible explanation for the exploding ovaries. After a few fraught weeks, further visits to doctors and more tests, I was given the all clear to continue treatment. I was focused on the moment and did not give the DES further thought.

But the end of August saw another failed attempt, with dwindling enthusiasm from all around for the next two cycles scheduled for September and October. Wondering why I wasn't getting pregnant, I was referred to a more specialist private hospital along the coast in Eastbourne. I had scans done to see if my one remaining ovary was still functioning. All seemed well. Reassured by more doctors I tried to stay positive for the next attempts. Big deep breaths and lots of positive thinking, but there was no blue line in September 1990, either and all of a sudden it was my last attempt. Could it be sixth time lucky? In October 1990 my six months were up and I had to return to Scotland and go back to work.

Nothing. A big fat nothing.

I couldn't believe it.

After all the determination to access fertility treatment, the patronising doctors, the move to London, taking time off work, being broke, my time was up. I wasn't pregnant. I was heartbroken as I made plans to return to Scotland.

I moved back and tried to pick up the threads of my life. You were still there in my imagination and my dreams, but during the day I threw myself back into work and politics. I had little idea what I could do next. Everyone was disappointed, the clinic, your Nana and Papa, my friends. I felt like a complete failure. Was that it, I wondered? My chance of motherhood, gone?

As things couldn't get any worse, I decided very reluctantly to contact Dr. C. again and made an appointment. My mum came with me to the hospital in all her finery to provide her nursing experience as reinforcement, as she knew how to handle doctors. We took along the copies of the scans that had been done at the private hospital in Eastbourne, which apparently showed some remnants of a second ovary. We wanted to know why I had not become pregnant on six occasions. Despite my mother's presence and her air of authority, he tossed these scan results across the table. '*That is not possible, I have had my hands in your abdomen and I know what is there.*' It appeared that I had some scraps of internal organs which existed in England, but somehow miraculously disappeared as I crossed the border into Scotland and the world controlled by Dr C. He was of course not in the least sympathetic that the treatment had not worked and he set his face against any further assistance with my fertility. However, he drew a distinction with medical intervention and after some strong persuasion from me, he finally agreed to admit me to hospital for a laparoscopy on 29th November 1990, to check the state of my one remaining ovary and tube. He agreed to this as a medical procedure as it was not directly connected to fertility treatment. Following this further operation, I was advised that all seemed okay and a further smear came back normal. So my existing half measures appeared to be in working order with no explanation for six failed cycles.

I returned to Women's Aid for Christmas with memories of what had happened two years before in the forefront of my mind. I tried to immerse myself in work, helping the women and children in the refuges and throwing myself head-first back into Labour Party politics. I was out at meetings every night of the week and at fundraising socials at weekends. But it was no good. I had started something, a journey into the unknown towards a distant land called motherhood. I was not ready to accept that it was all over. Deep down, I knew that I would only accept life without children if I had tried everything possible to make you happen. My New Year's resolution for 1991 was to return to London and more fertility treatment as soon as possible. Nothing else mattered. I handed in my resignation, worked my notice and arranged to move to London permanently. There was no going back.

So, January 1991 saw the start of another chapter and another journey south. If I wanted to be a mother, then I had to leave Scotland. I knew I had made the right decision. My family and friends weren't so sure, especially my feminist friends who thought I had gone completely mad. Giving everything up to have a baby, they muttered between themselves, but I knew. Baby-mad they thought. I tried to explain but saw perplexed stares looking back at me and after heated arguments about the existence or otherwise of the maternal instinct. I gave up trying to convince anyone else. It did not need to matter or make *any* sense, I decided, to anyone else but me. This was my life and my choice. Only I could take responsibility for my own destiny and I was going back to London.

I packed up what I could and put other boxes in storage. I hired a white van and your Uncle Colin agreed to drive me to London. All was arranged to start treatment again at BPAS in March 1991.

As I settled in London again, I realised that this time I would need to find a job quickly, so I signed on with a social work agency. Before I had time to catch my breath, I was working for the London Borough of Tower Hamlets which was as far away from any of my previous experience of social work as I could possibly imagine. The advantage of doing agency work was that I only got paid for the days I worked and I could take time off when I needed, so it was very flexible for plotting dates and treatment cycles. Clever me, I thought, I am in London again with no time restraints, so just relax and all will be well. I would talk to you in quiet moments convincing myself that by sheer determination I would achieve motherhood.

Then the outside world threatened to derail our destiny. My life was heading like a speeding train into an oncoming furore about single parents. The tabloid newspapers had run a story about a single woman having a baby. Trouble was that this particular mother attracted headlines about a later day virgin birth as she had had two children without ever having had sex. There was uproar. Unusually, even the Guardian editorial of 12th March 1991 was outraged. The editor condemned this woman asking how she was going to teach her children about sex and relationships. This editor then joined forces with one Dr. John Hobgood, Archbishop of York, in condemning wilful single parents highlighting the difficulties faced by their children. The Guardian, the bible of the middle class social work brigade, was donning the mantle of the reactionary right. Whatever next, I thought, having just moved to London, I resolved to keep my head down while sending positive vibes to my one sad ovary. I wanted a baby and yes, in the process I was going against the prevailing orthodoxy of the bishops and the newspapers, but what the hell did they know, bunch of misogynists. I decided that I would treat them with the contempt *they* deserved. I was furious with the Guardian but I wasn't campaigning, I was trying to live my life with the hand that I had been dealt.

This furore was whipped up at the beginning of March 1991. I have kept lots of newspaper cuttings. There is a big file of papers waiting for you. At the end of the very same month in 1991, I received a letter from BPAS confirming that my next cycle of treatment would go ahead and begin in April. Breathing a huge sigh of relief, I was reassured that BPAS was weathering the storm of all the press and negative publicity. I focused upon getting healthy ahead of the next cycle of treatment. Seventh time lucky, I hoped.

Sadly, not.

Once again, April 1991, brought just one more cycle of disappointment in a hostile world which was simultaneously dining out on their collective hatred of single parents. There was not much sympathy for me beyond my immediate friends and family and even they were becoming increasingly perplexed. By this time, I had learned not to expect much tea and sympathy. Treading this path meant that I had to develop the skin of a rhinoceros and adopt a healthy disrespect for archbishops, tabloid newspapers, and even the editor of the Guardian. I kept trying to be brave and courageous, but it was increasingly difficult.

When my friend Isobel came to visit me in London, we went for the day to Covent Garden. We sat there having lunch, in the midst of street theatre and happy tourists. Surrounded by the trappings of busy London, I felt profoundly sad. I seldom allowed myself to feel the crushing disappointment and the desperate fear of never having you. I would not allow this to end badly. I would not have a sad ending. I would not.

Another failed cycle, number eight, in May 1991 made motherhood seem like an impossible, unreachable goal; like space travel, winning the pools or finding a cure for cancer. It was, for me, somehow just impossible.

Deflated, I took myself off on a holiday by myself to rest my weary ovary.

I returned from holiday to receive a letter from BPAS dated 6th June 1991. Let's name and shame: Mr. Ian Jones, Director of BPAS announced that the clinic was closing down its sub-fertility service to *"Focus resources on its primary purpose of helping women facing unwanted and unplanned pregnancy."*

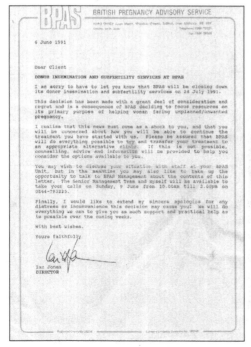

In other words, BPAS was concentrating its resources on terminating pregnancies rather than creating them. This was some twisted logic to abate the moral outrage of the right accepting that somehow abortions were better than single parents. I received this letter after eight unsuccessful cycles of fertility treatment. Sorry, it told me, but we are closing our doors to women who want to become pregnant. Mr. Jones did sign off with a flourish and a heartfelt apology for any distress or inconvenience. He had at least placated the archbishop. The BPAS clinic in Brighton was due to close down the fertility clinic in July 1991.

My last cycle of treatment in June 1991 took place in a state of complete disbelief. I had relocated to London, started as a social worker in Tower Hamlets, travelled to and from the South Coast of England to clinics in Brighton and Eastbourne, all to no avail. *'Where next,'* I wondered, *'America perhaps?'* This ninth cycle of treatment was our last chance and I hoped with every bone in my body that you would make your presence felt before it was too late. But yet again, that cycle was unsuccessful and ended with the loud bang of another door behind me. This time shut for good.

In a rather guilty afterthought, the Guardian printed another article in June 1991 entitled 'Motherhood made harder', toning down their previous outrage and adopting a new editorial line implying that the range of a woman's sexual experience did not affect her ability to be a good parent. Sorry, Mr. Editor, much too little and much too late. I was cast adrift, with my one ovary putting away with no baby in sight.

Meanwhile, I was spending my day job as a social worker in Tower Hamlets Social Services, dealing with child abuse and neglect. This was increasingly hard. It was so difficult seeing the neglect and abuse of children first hand when I was so desperate to be a mother myself. I remember one particular afternoon, I had gone on a home visit to a young mother whose three year old son and baby daughter were at risk. She just didn't have the resources to cope; in care herself, she had graduated to a council flat, early unplanned pregnancies and a life of poverty and deprivation visited on the next generation. (By the way, any politician who ever comes near me and smugly suggests this is some sort of career plan, from wanton teenager to impoverished motherhood, will get two black eyes for his trouble).

That afternoon, I stood outside that council flat after another home visit with such a feeling of hopelessness and despair for that family and for me. What, I asked myself, could one individual social worker visiting a couple of times a week really do to change their plight? Not bloody much. I stood on the balcony of this council block in Tower Hamlets, wondering what the hell I could do. It was one of those big imposing council estates that often featured on TV programs like *The Bill* with long corridors and balconies outside each row of flats. It was the most surreal experience, as the area was under redevelopment with Canary Wharf and the Docklands nearby. But the compulsory purchase orders had not managed to recover all the land, so the council blocks were sandwiched among new deluxe apartments and posh yacht clubs disguising the pockets of poverty which existed in their reflection.

Very briefly, as I stood overlooking this scene of poverty, yacht clubs and confused humanity, I seriously contemplated going back into the flat and taking those kids. Just taking them and running like hell, giving them some chance of a better life, like some desperado infertile social worker trying to do some good in a bleak and unfair world. Of course, I didn't, as I also didn't want to end up in Holloway Prison or spend my life on the run with two kids. But the fact that it even crossed my mind sent a shiver down my spine. I needed to seriously get a grip, if I couldn't have you, then I couldn't continue being a social worker seeing other children suffer.

I had no idea what to do next. My whole life seemed to have turned upside down and was unravelling before my eyes.

The following story appeared in Spare Rib in July 1991.

BPAS Ends Donor Insemination

On Friday June 7th 1991, all the women making use of the Donor Insemination and Subfertility Clinic at the British Pregnancy Advisory Service (BPAS) received a short letter telling them that the service would be ending on July 26th.

BPAS, which was recently at the centre of the 'Virgin Births' story seized upon by the tabloids early this year says that their decision has nothing to do with this, but is being made because they want to 'concentrate their resources on women facing unplanned/unwanted pregnancies.'

The reason they are giving for terminating the service to women already on the programme, is that they feel the service is adequately provided elsewhere.

BPAS, long seen by feminists as a pro-women clinic, is one of the very few prepared to provide a donor insemination service to single women. It will be very hard for women to find an alternative. And the decision to end the insemination programme while it is in progress must make women doubt BPAS 's ability to act in a caring way in the other services provide.

Many of the changes at BPAS seem to have come about since the present director, Ian Jones, took over. He is known to have come in with a 'business like attitude' towards running the service, determined to make it financially viable. Insemination and fertility advice is more expensive to provide than abortion advice, and this is undoubtedly one of the reasons why the decision to cut the service was made.

The decision has also been influenced by the political climate. It is interesting that the 'Virgin Births' story broke when it did. BPAS has in fact been providing an insemination service to lesbians and single women for about ten years so the information was hardly 'new', but it was nicely timed to influence those sitting on the working party for the Human Embryology White Paper which is expected to report in the summer. It would seem that the whole thing has been carefully orchestrated by those who disagree with insemination of single women.

So, politics, news opportunism and scaremongering, finance and high-handed management have all combined to leave an unknown number high and dry in the middle of a treatment they had expected to continue until conception, or at least until the service was outlawed. Yet another nail in the coffin for women - whether they live outside of the conventional nuclear family or not - who want to have the right to control their own fertility. And of course, all the women who worked in the service all over Britain, will, from the end of July, have no job.

Write in protest against the termination of the service to Ian Jones, Director, BPAS, Austy Manor, Wootton Wawen, Solihull, West Midlands B95 6BX

Chapter 9

During my treatment at Brighton, I had been having scans at a private hospital in Eastbourne to check that I was ovulating, the scan results Dr C had tossed back across his desk. With the clinic in Brighton closed, I contacted the doctor in Eastbourne to see if I could be accepted for further fertility treatment along the coast.

The appointment was arranged at the Esperance Hospital for Tuesday 25th June 1991. Understandably, given my previous experiences, I approached this further consultation with some anxiety. To my relief the doctor who greeted me seemed friendly. He smiled and welcomed me into his office. As soon as he said, *'Hello.'* and *'Please sit down,'* I realised that he had a Scottish accent. How weird, I thought, here I am in Eastbourne at the very South of England and I meet another Scottish Doctor. Dr R.

Dr. R proceeded to tell me that he had read all my notes with interest and that he had in fact previously worked in Scotland as a colleague of Dr. C. I was astounded. Could my luck get any worse? There I was, at a hospital practically in France, with nine failed cycles, moral outrage, angry Archbishops and a closed BPAS clinic behind me, only to find myself staring at a Scottish gynaecologist friend of the 'don't have babies out of wedlock' Dr. C. My heart truly sank. I was stunned into silence. Talk about bad karma, I just sat there, lost for words.

There seemed little point pandering to further prejudice, no matter how desperate I felt. I refused to debase myself, refused to lose my dignity or integrity by crying uncontrollably and throwing myself upon his mercy. I looked him in the eye and slowly and calmly asked him if I was wasting my time.

If ever there was a moment to change my life, it was that afternoon when I made the acquaintance of a kind, truly non-judgmental, humane doctor who looked at me sympathetically for once, regardless of the seething outrage of bishops and newspapers, and agreed to accept me for fertility treatment. Most unlikely to sue, this wonderful doctor truly deserves his full name – Mr. David Robertson.

Following further medical examinations, scans, blood tests and, as the Americans would say, a complete workup, I was accepted for treatment at the Esperance Hospital in Eastbourne. This was to be a whole new ballgame. Putting the nine failed, risk averse, drug free cycles behind me, I embarked on a high tech intervention and a much more expensive regime where my one and only remaining ovary was to be shocked out of its complacency. I would be pumped full of hormones. Higher risks were stressed and understood. The possibility of multiple pregnancy could not be ruled out and there were risks associated with the powerful drugs. I did not hear any of that, I nodded and signed the forms as all I heard, was an offer of help and renewed hope. I was not quite at the end of the road. I was by this stage thirty and a half.

High tech, high risk, high hopes and high cost. I had graduated to the next level of being a fertility patient. Now, I really needed to find serious full time work quickly to finance this more expensive treatment. I had been looking for other jobs, moving away from social work and the risks of kidnapping neglected kids, trying for more political and campaigning roles. As well as working as an agency social worker I had applied for a few jobs in London, like MP's researchers, campaigning groups and had had an unsuccessful interview to be a trade union official with NUPE.

Although I was focused on earning money and paying my own way, any honest account of my fertility treatment and living in London must mention the generous financial support of my hardworking parents. Cycle after cycle they helped me pay for treatment and survive in London. Any nest egg they had put away for their retirement was generously and unconditionally given to try to assist one of my eggs to

76

become a pregnancy and possibly their first grandchild. This was single parent pregnancy by collective family effort.

My dad's resolve weakened a few times after the many tearful phone calls telling of failed cycles. After one particularly upsetting conversation he threatened to get on the train to London and drag me back to Motherwell. Enough was enough, he said. My mum, though equally worried, took a more practical medical approach and was pleased that this new hospital was going to help, telling me not to worry about the cost. My ovary exhausted their retirement savings. In theory, at least, they should also have the poshest kitchen in West Central Scotland as they applied for bank loan after bank loan under the guise of a new fitted kitchen. Between us, we managed to pay for the drug treatments and, with much excitement and anticipation, I started treatment cycle number ten at the Esperance Hospital in July 1991.

My remaining ovary had been hyper stimulated with powerful drugs to produce more eggs. I was scanned and monitored and, finally, when the time was right, IUI (Intra-Uterine Insemination) involved a long catheter to try to ensure that the egg and sperm were acquainted in the smallest possible space. Unlike the drug-free AID, it was not just a complete shot in the dark with fingers crossed. I was so excited, it was not just my ovary churning away, shocked into action by the drugs producing excess follicles, I was hyper stimulated on every front. This was it at last. The two week wait was utter purgatory.

Then, despite all the drugs and scans, the money and the posh hospital, nothing. Absolutely nothing. No blue line, no pink dot, not pregnant again. Ten times by now. Bloody hell. How hard could this be? The disappointment was so hard to take, I had to scrape myself off the floor, gather my resources, both financial and emotional, and look ahead to the next attempt. I had set off on this determined path and I was equally determined not to weaken or show my despair. Dealing with

77

disappointment became my forte. I was like one of these fat-bottomed dolls that get battered about but always bounce back for more. Weebles wobble but they don't fall down. Nor do feminists.

I was often low, but I refused to quit. It felt like an agonising roller coaster, with high peaks of excitement and deep ravines of despair in the space of a few weeks, all hopes would build up only to come crashing down. In my low moments, I would think, '*Fuck's sake I really don't know how much more of this I can endure.*' But to me it was important not to let the rest of the world see just how hard it was, I had to keep an invincible exterior as I didn't want to upset my mum and dad anymore, but I really was not sure how much more I could bear. Simone was the one person who saw and understood. Despite her own difficulties with being a single parent, she never tried to dissuade me from carrying on. At that time we were a mutual support system as we tried to face the trials and tribulations of each day.

Don't look back, I told myself. Face forwards and prepare for the next cycle.

It was by now August 1991, with more fertility treatment and more drugs for the next cycle. I made trips up and down to Eastbourne from Victoria Station after work or days off as required. I got quite blasé about getting across London on the tube to Victoria Station and on the train for one and a three quarter hours down to Eastbourne, doing the reverse journey, if possible, the same evening. If things didn't go to plan, I would book into a bed and breakfast or hotel in Eastbourne. What with my previous trips to Brighton, I became very well acquainted with Victoria Station and the South Coast of England. Unlike most Scots, I have a very soft spot for London and the South of England.

Treatment cycle number eleven brought the usual stuff: drugs, excitement, more money, scans and absolutely loads of merry follicles. I received very stern lectures about multiple pregnancy and the risk of hyper-stimulation syndrome, hence the late night trips two or three nights a week, to and from Eastbourne from London for scans. Finally, the day of treatment and ovulation arrived. Then the hideous wait where two weeks feels like twenty years. Then? Nothing, failed again, absolutely bloody nothing. No baby, no blue line, no foetus, not even a tadpole. Nothing, just nothing. Jesus. How could this be?

This was not just devastating, it was embarrassing. I felt as though I was malformed, disabled, not working properly. Yet, I was at my fittest. I had not had a drop of alcohol for three years. I was a size ten, taking my folic acid tablets, vitamins, the works. I had even gone to alternative practitioners in trendy Stoke Newington and been prescribed the most foul herbal tea imaginable. I was determined to maximise my chance and do what I could to get pregnant. I was assured all along that I had acquired grade A sperm which was all washed and lovely. So what the hell was the problem? I was an embarrassed, angry failure, getting older by the minute. I tried to talk nicely to my one remaining ovary but I wanted to scream. *I WANT A BABY!* Instead I had to get up and get on with making a living to pay all the bills for the failed pregnancies, like I'd paid well over the odds each month to have my period.

Fertility treatment is like a rollercoaster or, perhaps more accurately, like a heart attack chart with great peaks and troughs of hope and disappointment. So in September 1991, I sighed but started my twelfth cycle of treatment. I asked Dr. Robertson how long this should go on for and he advised that it was time to consider GIFT and IVF. The distinction between different assisted conception techniques gets lost in tabloid headlines where all treatment is misunderstood under the banner of IVF. GIFT then was an intermediate step where the eggs are collected the same way but replaced in the fallopian tube with the sperm before conception to try to encourage natural conception within the confines of the fallopian tube followed by natural (drug assisted) implantation. So I went

79

through the motions with my twelfth, last IUI cycle with powerful drugs, in September 1991 and signed up for GIFT due to start the week beginning 28th October 1991. Just to be counter intuitive I thought it was bound to be thirteenth time lucky.

This was pregnancy by Filofax. I was impatient for my next cycle to start so that I could predict the date, arrange the scan, organise time off work. I was willing the usual horrible two week wait to end, to be over with, for my hugely expensive period to start so that I could plan ahead for the next cycle.

That weekend, I was alone in the flat as Simone had taken Elliott away to her mum's. My mum was on holiday in Ireland with my granny visiting Auntie Annie, my grandpa's sister. Don't be fooled by tales of the good old days and how families used to be sitting around the table playing "happy families" while tucking into delicious meals together. One of five children my grandpa and his brothers and sisters were taken on holiday as young children to visit relatives in Ireland, during which time Annie, aged five, caught scarlet fever and was too ill to travel home back to Scotland. So they just left her there with relatives to get better. But then, for whatever strange reason, they never ever went back for her and young Annie grew up in Ireland. She married but was never able to have any children. My mum visited her regularly especially after she became an elderly widow living alone in rural Ireland. This time, she had taken my Nana along for a holiday.

I had just finished another week of inner city social work. I took to my bed exhausted. Lifting my diary to check my dates for the next cycle, I thought I had made some mistake. If my period did not get a move, on I would not be able to start the drugs for the GIFT cycle and the dates for October would need to be completely rearranged. '*Oh, bloody hell. Nothing is going right,*' I thought. I decided to sleep on it, determined to sort it all out in the morning. I felt utterly weary.

Next morning, I woke up to a very quiet flat with no tell-tale signs of cramp or any sort of activity down below whatsoever. A very creepy feeling started to tingle all over my body. *'What on earth did this mean? Was I just late? What should I do?'* I would not let any thoughts, any possibility of you or pregnancy enter my head. I pushed hope away. I crawled out of bed in a trance, pulled on some clothes and made my way to the local chemist in Dalston. I bought every make and colour of pregnancy test I could find. Pink dots, blue lines, zig zags, you name it, I bought every one. Then I crawled back to the flat.

I was so nervous unwrapping the cellophane. I peed for Britain on each test and then ran out of the bathroom back to bed and hid under the covers. Tick tock. Three minutes later, I apprehensively opened the door of the bathroom and looked at the little rows of plastic tests on top of the cistern. There to my utter amazement, right in front of my very own eyes, was a pink line and a blue dot. I grabbed the instruction sheet. I was pregnant.

Pregnant? Really? Really? No – really, I was hysterical!

I ran quickly back to bed and lay down again, doing deep breathing exercises, I propped pillows under my bum until I was nearly upside down and all the blood was rushing to my head. I just couldn't believe it. I managed to pull the phone nearer the bed to phone my mum in Ireland. Your Nana remembers to this day that hysterical phone call. *'It's me, it's pink, it's pink ... it's bloody pink.'*

My mum was delighted of course but she told me later that when she put the phone down in the hall and went back into the living room to tell her elderly Aunt Annie and my Nana, she took a deep breath and warned my grannie not to say a word. Not a single word. She then told them that I was pregnant.

My Catholic granny put the tea towel over her head and rocked back and forth.

'Jesus, Mary and Joseph.'

'Jesus, Mary and Joseph.'

'Jesus, Mary and Joseph.'

Auntie Annie, Irish and Catholic with no kids of her own, said *'Good for her,'* and poured them all a stiff drink.

Twelfth time lucky! You had finally made your presence felt and I was overjoyed.

But at the same time, I could not allow myself to believe it. I did not want to stand up or get out of bed for fear that the few blobs of my hugely expensive, dividing cells giving rise to this surge in hormones, might just drop out and/or be peed carelessly away down a toilet in Hackney. This was you, our precious Scottish child and grandchild, and I was going to do everything possible to hold on to you.

So for the whole weekend I lay still in bed, alone, not moving, not allowing myself to eat, only getting up to the toilet in a very quiet deserted flat. I was completely still and alone praying intensely that this was finally it. With brazen hypocrisy I entered into solemn pacts with God that, despite my failure as a Catholic, I was a good person. I would be a good mother. I would do good things with my life if he just let this be true. I prayed and slept for two full days, hoping against hope for a healthy baby in nine months' time.

Although I had spent a small fortune on pregnancy testing kits from the chemist, I also arranged to have a blood test at the hospital. I took the day off on the Monday, making my way very tentatively across London on the tube to Victoria Station and then the train down to Eastbourne. The blood test was taken and then I had to wait two days for the result. Dr. Robertson called me on Thursday, 26th September 1991 with the magical words, *'I am delighted to confirm that you are pregnant.'*

There was singing and dancing on the streets of Hackney and Motherwell while I took to my bed.

Chapter 10

Curiously, perhaps subconsciously never expecting to get pregnant, I had agreed to go to Paris with a group of friends for Isobel's fortieth birthday in November 1991. I was also due to be chief bridesmaid to Linda, in October 1991 and had to fly up to Scotland for a dress fitting. I wasn't going to stay size ten for long, I thought.

The main feeling I remember from those first few weeks of pregnancy was disbelief, coupled with both secret fantasy and fear of multiple pregnancies. All the stern lectures and scans showing multiple follicles came rushing back but I had to wait six weeks for the first scan to establish whether I was to become a single mother par excellence of twins, triplets or even more. My mum arranged time off from the hospital, flew down to London and came with me for the first glimpse of you, her much wanted grandchild (or more?). Secretly, I wished for twins, no more, but twins, that would be okay. I would manage somehow. Above all, I wanted just to remain pregnant and I wanted you to be healthy.

When the day came, the scan revealed one tiny beating dot, one heartbeat right there on the screen. Your determined little spirit, against all the odds was causing the tiniest of blips on the screen but the biggest rollercoaster of emotions, hopes and fears in London and in Scotland. After all this time it was true. It was real. I could hardly contain myself. I wanted to tell the whole world and had to try hard to wait until the risky time after twelve weeks had passed. But then, mostly everyone knew why I had moved to London and would ask the question. I could not lie. It became a collective neurosis and anxiety. Finally would this stay true? I wanted to announce your conception to the world as soon as possible. The six o'clock news, a Paxman interview perhaps, '*Of course I am a feminist, Jeremy, and so delighted to be pregnant.*' Anything seemed possible.

83

So began nine months of excitement and anxiety, watching every morsel that passed my lips and taking absolutely nothing for granted. Linda's wedding was a huge challenge. There I was done up to the nines, by this time with blond hair covering the grey with a flowery tiara thing balanced on my head to match the bride, a green shiny bridesmaid frock, looking every bit the feminist in disguise. I had resolved to be low key as I was only just two months pregnant. And besides, it was Linda's big day. I was not drinking of course. My mum and dad were invited as parents of the bridesmaid and family friends. It was inevitable, I suppose, that after a couple of glasses of champagne, my mum could not contain her excitement and our "secret" was out. It caused something of a stir among the guests at this traditional Catholic wedding that the unmarried bridesmaid was pregnant having taken herself off to London for fertility treatment, but we were all so happy I don't remember any adverse comment and the bride, Linda, and her groom, Brian, didn't appear to have any problem with their somewhat controversial bridesmaid. After all, for my part, I had agreed to wear a silly frock and put flowers in my hair.

Bridesmaid at Linda's Wedding October 1991

Nine months passed with no major problems. My memories of being pregnant are of sitting in the café of Clissold Park in Stoke Newington consuming generous portions of carrot cake. I was so chuffed, I wanted my bump to show as soon as possible. I was eating heartily for two and wanted the world to know it.

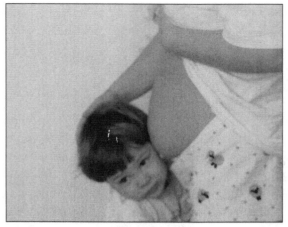

The Bump!

I decided to work only part-time as a social worker in Tower Hamlets. In November, with reassurances from Dr Robertson, I flew to Paris, having flown up to Scotland to meet my friends and then to Paris via Birmingham. I have a photograph of me, still looking thin with the middle cut out of a pancake which had arrived at the table with fried egg in the middle. No eggs - no alcohol still - but only regular food quelled the constant nausea. Throughout my pregnancy, I had to have three breakfasts. In Paris I found a baby shop along a back street and nervously bought a very expensive but tiny babygro with feet. As I did not know whether you would be a boy or a girl I chose a pale turquoise with lemon bunny rabbits. It was adorable. But I was then so gripped with fear that I had somehow tempted fate, I hid the fancy parcel at the very bottom of my suitcase.

In December 1991, I was godmother to Elliot who was by

now one and a half. We travelled down to his grandmother's and there was a very simple Christening in a tiny Dorset village church, St Michaels Church in Stinsford, followed by singing round the piano, back at his gran's house with lots of family and friends. His gran Carol was head of Dorset Youth Orchestra, and Elliott was soon to inherit her musical gifts and also become fluent in French. But I am getting ahead of myself. I will tell more about Elliott later on.

Singing Christmas Carols around the piano in Dorset all seemed like a fairy tale much removed from life in inner city Hackney, and there was I in the middle of it all, a pregnant Scottish feminist. Funny how life works out, I thought. I have very happy pictures of me at this time, looking after Elliott and looking forward to a whole new chapter of life, full of children.

Christening and Christmas in Dorset

When I went home to Scotland for Christmas, I was on cloud nine and must still have been on my early pregnancy eating binge. When I returned to London in January 1992 and was back at work, another social worker remarked that my mother must have fed me too many Christmas dinners as I hadn't half put on lots of weight! Finally the bump was official. I was ecstatic. I announced safely after the three months that I was pregnant. Surprise and good wishes followed. No adverse comments. After all, this was London, where anything goes. I felt happy and supported amongst the diversity of life and lifestyles that London embraces.

I worked three days a week and spent the other two days helping the local MP, Diane Abbott. I helped out in her office and assisted with her surgery. She was then the only black female MP in the House of Commons and had recently had her baby son. The community of Hackney couldn't have been more diverse and different from Scotland. The politics of the Labour Party in London and in Hackney were interesting to say the least, a dramatic contrast to the Edinburgh and Lanarkshire branches and constituencies I had been used to.

Naturally, your Nana and Papa were wondering whether I would move back to Scotland and my flat in Hamilton. At that stage, I just wasn't sure. I enjoyed the diversity and anonymity of London life. In the trendy part of North London I inhabited, I had met a wealth of different people where any combination of alternative lifestyle seemed not just possible, but fashionable and desirable. Given the hostility I had already experienced north of the border, I wasn't sure that I wanted to return back to Scotland to have you, my much wanted baby, stigmatised. My priority for the time being was to remain pregnant and have you in the supportive atmosphere of cosmopolitan London.

About eighteen months earlier, I had applied for a job as a trade union official with NUPE in London. It was a long shot, but I knew I wanted to move away from social work and dealing daily with abused and neglected children. I was shortlisted and interviewed but had not been offered the job. Now pregnant, still mulling over my long-term plans, I saw the same job advertised again in the Guardian but decided to do nothing as my circumstances had changed. I wasn't sure if I would stay long term in London or not. One morning in March 1992, quite unsolicited, a letter dropped onto the mat inviting me to reapply for this new vacancy as I had only narrowly failed to be appointed last time. Interesting karma I thought, so I filled in the forms and posted them off with my only true concern and focus being pregnancy and motherhood.

This approach seemed to do the trick, as I was invited to an interview to become a trade union official with NUPE, the National Union of Public Employees. Then the 1992 election was called and the interviews were postponed, as all resources were geared up to fighting the election that was finally going to get rid of the Tories. Although now heavily pregnant, I was very involved in the local constituency campaign for Diane Abbott and stayed up all night in a state of denial and despair as it became clear that my much longed-for baby was going to be born under another Tory government. I took the 1992 election defeat of the Labour Party very personally indeed.

The day after the election, I remember going into a flower shop in Dalston. I decided to buy myself some flowers to cheer myself up. I must have looked like a desolate figure as the woman in the shop came over to me. *'Never mind dear, it looks as though you don't have long to go now.'* I explained at some length to this woman that my depression and despair were not about being pregnant, but about my baby being born under a Conservative government. I was very happy to be pregnant as I had tried for a long time to have a baby, but I really wanted a Labour government too.

She stared back at me puzzled, then helped me pick out a lovely bunch of flowers while remarking that her life, my life and my baby's life would not change one little bit, no matter what kind of government we had. It was always just the same for us, she said, no matter who ran the country. I appreciated her kindness to me that day, but I so wanted her to be wrong. I had grown up under the Tories since I was eighteen. I had so wanted Labour to win the election, for a new political chapter to begin, just as my own life was about to change forever. But in 1992, I had to settle for a large bunch of flowers as compensation and some sad but friendly words from a woman who clearly felt politicians made no difference to her life at all.

Finally, the job interview was rearranged following the election defeat. In the circumstances, it was more of a wake than an interview. By this time, I was now thirty-eight weeks pregnant with you and the size of a London bus. Back then, Mothercare did not have a section for interview suits for the woman only two weeks away from giving birth. There was no hiding the fact that I was enormously pregnant. So, after careful thought, I opted for the bold choice of a very baggy red, orange and white psychedelic long maternity blouse with matching red leggings and red lipstick. I cannot recall the colour of my hair by this time, highlights I think, as I attempted to hide the post-thirty grey. I was quite a sight to behold, massive, colourful and very pregnant.

I remember the day of the interview, which involved individual interviews and group discussions. I arrived in my over-the-top psychedelic pregnancy ensemble to find a room full of sombre suited and booted individuals who failed in any effort to hide their contempt and amusement at the sight of my colourful, pregnant self, waddling into a very formal boardroom in Holborn. Then when we were asked to introduce ourselves, my Scottish accent reinforced the other applicants' assessment that I was the token (pregnant) woman with no hope of getting the job. Smug smiles washed around the room like a Mexican wave as the other candidates reassessed their odds.

Amazingly enough, for my part, I really did not give a shit. I was relaxed and happy. I had other things on my mind. I had made the effort to get myself there and to look presentable, so I was going to have a good time. I was interviewed by two trade union officials now sitting comfortably in the House of Lords, Lord Tom Sawyer and Baroness Maggie Jones. Thinking that I had nothing to lose, I was at my outspoken best and at least I stood out from the other candidates. To my amazement, I was offered the job and negotiated a starting date of January 1993 to allow me six months off with my baby.

Hey, finally I was on a roll. A job in London, and a baby, I was going to rule the world, after all.

During my antenatal appointments, all was going well and I was referred to a Natural Childbirth Trust (NCT) yoga class to help deal with breathing and anxiety. Not that I had any intentions of any natural childbirth nonsense. No way. Drug assisted conception followed by drug fuelled labour was my straightforward uncomplicated birth plan. Nevertheless, I went along to classes with the most middle class group of women I had ever encountered in the one place at the one time. There we all were, waddling about, dressed in leggings and baggy t-shirts, swapping stories, comparing bumps as the weeks progressed, ending each session with some healthy but vile smelling herbal tea.

I could not really get into the yoga wholeheartedly, I never shared their confidence that at the end of this adventure an elusive healthy baby would actually appear (even though I was as wide as I was tall). I did treat myself to a weekly massage with an aromatherapist, carefully avoiding all the stronger oils banned during pregnancy as I anticipated my due date and your arrival on 25th May 1992.

Despite my previous medical problems and operations, not to mention the difficult journey to getting pregnant, those nine months were bliss with very few problems. Except for one incident, when friends from Scotland were in London visiting and we went out for a pizza in Islington. I had felt fine all day but all of a sudden I told them that I didn't feel very well. Next thing I knew I was spark out, on the floor of the restaurant moaning and groaning with a fork down my throat. Some bright person had heard that to avoid the danger of choking, a fork should be used to prevent the person swallowing their own tongue. I was so embarrassed when I came round, that I actually sat there trying to finish the pizza and wouldn't allow anyone to call an ambulance. But as soon as I got back to the flat, I was on the phone to Accident and Emergency, crying my eyes out as the nurse asked how long I had been unconscious. Imagine losing my baby over a pizza and a fork. Fortunately, my pregnancy memories mostly involve looking after Elliott. We also had a glorious summer in 1992, I had stopped work and spent my time pushing Elliott in his buggy around Clissold Park and visiting the animals. We also watched endless Disney videos. Elliott's favourite was always *The Little Mermaid*. As we watched all the Disney cartoons I experimented in my head with alternative names, as I quite liked Sebastian and Anastasia.

But my due date came and went. Your Nana arranged time off work and came down to London again. She fussed about, wanting to change the curtains in Simone's flat and cleaning endlessly. She found her way around Dalston Market and made sure we had everything ready and prepared. Still nothing happened. The waiting and the tension became unbearable. After a week, I was ready to try desperate measures and booked a further massage with orders to slap on all the contraband aromatherapy oils in North London. Afterwards, I arranged to meet your Nana across the road from the health centre in a coffee come jazz bar in Stoke Newington's Church Street and within twenty minutes the contractions started around 5:30 pm on Monday, 1st June 1992. My bag had been packed for a week and as I had a bath, my waters broke. How well planned, I thought, and hoped the rest would be equally straight forward. I should have known.

We finally arrived at Homerton Hospital, Hackney at 9:30 that night. True to form, nothing much went to plan, apart from the request to keep the drugs coming thick and fast. You were in distress, and I was attached to all sorts of monitors, was violently sick and after a gruelling time, I took my revenge on the medical profession in spectacular fashion. I haemorrhaged, splattering blood all over the nurses and doctor in attendance while family history repeated itself as large forceps yanked you, my baby daughter, into the world at 6:30 am on 2nd June 1992. This was the pinnacle of my powers, the invincible feminist achieved motherhood at last and a healthy baby daughter. I was both ecstatic and exhausted.

You were small but perfect, just six pounds in weight, but perfectly healthy and well. Your Nana, now officially a grandmother at last (although exhausted too), was dispatched to buy smaller first size clothes for premature babies for the first official photograph. We couldn't have this first long awaited photograph with my baby in outsized clothes, rolled up at the sleeves with the feet dangling empty. You had to be perfect and perfectly dressed. And you were in every way.

Colin duly arrived at the hospital in Hackney having forsaken Mothercare. Instead, he came with a carrier bag full of newspapers, from the Morning Star to the Daily Telegraph, just to ensure that his first born niece would have a record of world events and politics on the day of her birth. We still have those newspapers and your tiny baby clothes to this day in the trunk with your baby photographs.

Meanwhile in Scotland, my dad had answered the phone at 6.45 am to be told that he was a grandfather. My mum was with me in London, so he cried and celebrated alone. Despite all his initial reservations, later that day, my dad, now your Papa, bought a round of drinks for his friends at the golf club proud of the achievements of his single parent daughter and ecstatic at your arrival, his very first grandchild.

Chapter 11

This hospital experience, in the maternity ward with you, felt like no other. I was in hospital for two days and I felt like a superstar, powerful beyond belief. Flowers and congratulations arrived by the dozen. Despite the major transfusion of eight pints of blood, the twelve hour labour and the emotional rollercoaster of giving birth to you, my perfect six-pound baby girl, the nurses thought it was just a great idea and perfectly routine to deliver you in your new pink babygro to the side of my bed in a see through plastic Moses basket, while they attended to other patients and would be mothers. There you were, right beside me, forever.

Although exhausted and desperate for sleep, I could only stare at you, my little bundle of new life. I could not believe you were here safe and well and so perfect in every respect. You had thick dark hair. Colin remarked that you looked like a wee hamster, crouched up, eating your fists. I thought you were the most miraculous little creature I had ever seen in my entire life. I could not take my eyes off of you, nor dare to sleep.

What if this was all a dream, I thought ? What if there had been some mix up and some other mother came to claim you, '*Ha, ha, not yours, you must be joking ... or ... the HFEA don't think it is a very good idea ... we want to give her to a good two parent family.*'

You need to understand that at the very same time during the eighties and early nineties, as I was losing parts of my reproductive anatomy, and was engaged on my own personal fertility journey, politicians were increasingly interested in regulating the scientific advances in assisted conception and also legislating for who should and should not be allowed access to fertility treatment. They were very busy making the personal political in relation to fertility treatment in private clinics and hospitals in the UK.

The Human Fertilisation and Embryology Bill was given a second reading in the House of Lords in December 1989. The debates in Parliament focused on three main issues: embryo research, welfare of the child, and abortion. The Bill received Royal Assent on 1st November 1990, with the HFEA taking up its full statutory responsibilities in August 1991. While the Act contained a number of prohibitions on the uses of human embryos, it also gave wide powers of interpretation to the HFEA. The Act set out the duties of the HFEA, including the requirement to publish a Code of Practice and maintain a register of those receiving treatment and born as a result of treatment.

So the timing of these legislative and political changes meant that any pregnancies as a result of assisted conception, after August 1991, had to be officially registered with the state. It so happens that my twelfth cycle of treatment was finally successful very soon after the dawn of this officialdom in September 1991, which meant that the state, under the auspices at that time the Tory government officially recorded my positive pregnancy test, and nine months later registered your birth with the HFEA.

At the same time as I was receiving baby cards and bouquets of flowers upon the birth of my longed-for baby, some civil servant somewhere was adding our names to a new list, to ensure that the great and the good on the Human Fertilisation and Embryology Authority paid attention to your welfare and any others born through assisted conception. Ignoring their misplaced concern, I noted that, much like an adoption register, you could make contact with the HFEA when you reached eighteen, but I also wondered where the state's concern was for the welfare of the many neglected children still living in Tower Hamlets and on another register entirely – the "at risk" register.

As you were born in June 1992, you are the very first generation of HFEA assisted conception statistics and one of the first ever children to be registered with the HFEA in the UK.

In hospital in June 1992, looking at you, my tiny new baby happily curled up and sleeping beside me, entirely dependent upon me and me alone, I determined that very minute to be the most vigilant mother in creation to ensure that you wanted for nothing. My approach to motherhood was to be invincible and determined from day one. The HFEA would have no cause to worry about your welfare, I would see to that.

However, at the same time I was weepy and hormonal. I was overjoyed, yet overwhelmed. I cried on and off for two days, managing to pull myself together only for visiting times. My previous matter of fact emotions, my brave face at not getting pregnant and multiple disappointments of the last two years engulfed me.

Yet, I was the happiest I had ever been in my life. The busy nurses smiled and explained that it was just my hormones, but I knew different. I had, after all the ups and downs, finally become a mother. With all the hostility and doubts that I had encountered along the way about my choice to be a single mother, I resolved not to waste any time doubting myself but resolved to be the best mother I could be to you, my precious baby.

Simone brought Elliott to visit us in the hospital. He had turned two in April and was very much used to having me all

95

to himself. I was his special 'Cargil'. He scrambled up onto the bed and wanted to hold you. We took lots of photographs of your first day together, like brother and new wee sister in a new alternative family. I was careful to make sure Elliott felt involved and the next day, we took more photographs as he helped me to carry the baby seat into the car, as we left Homerton Hospital to go home.

Your Nana had arranged annual leave from the hospital and so we went around London taking pictures, everywhere, hardly able to believe the new reality of our lives. Your baby photograph album has 'baby in sling first time on London bus', 'registering birth of first Scottish grandchild at Hackney Town Hall' and 'seeing Nana on train back to Scotland'. Nana was of course sad that I was not returning to Scotland with her, but I was very glad that I had a job lined up in six months' time. As part of this long fertility journey, I was putting down roots in London.

Despite my fantasy of names from Disney videos, my baby names had been chosen for a long time so that during my pregnancy we referred to my bump as Ben – Tasha. Keir Benjamin for a boy I thought, after Keir Hardie, but called Ben every day. Similarly, I had chosen Rosa Natasha for a girl who would be called Natasha. You know that you are named after Rosa Luxembourg and Rosa Parks, great feminist icons of their time. But I thought this was a tall order for you to live up to on a day to day basis so I decided on the unusual choice of your middle name as your everyday name, as well as your 'political' name. This is not something you have thanked me for as you changed teachers every year in primary school when you had to explain why your first name was Rosa but you are called Natasha, you would sigh and explain, ''*Cos my mum is a feminist, Miss.*'

Once out of hospital, our first "home" was still only Simone's spare room in Hackney, up four flights of stairs in a block of flats with no lift, off Amhurst Road. It was far from ideal. She made lots of changes to her flat, giving up her bigger room to give us more space, and I tried to organise things as much as possible in the small flat and keep things tidy. I didn't care about anything else but having a healthy baby. We settled into a routine as an informal alternative family. Simone was working part-time as a social worker at the children's hospital and I was on unpaid maternity leave between jobs. I did lots of housework and childcare. I looked after you and helped with toddler Elliott when he was not in nursery. He was besotted with you and not the least bit put out by the new arrival. All my baby albums have the two of you, playing together, being read bedtime stories, seeing Santa, in the park, on holiday by the sea.

I remember such a blissful time in those first six months.

Home from Hospital

It was a wonderfully special time, when I believed everything was possible and that I was truly invincible. Of course I was broke, but I was determined to provide for you. I looked to the future with immense hope. After all, I now had my baby, I had lined up a job in the new year and was enjoying the novelty of settling down in London.

Due to the fact that I had been an agency social worker, I had no maternity leave or pay until I started my new job, so I had to sign on to receive benefit for those six months. Bearing in mind that I had worked for the previous decade paying my taxes, and had none of my fertility treatment funded by the NHS, this was a purely short term measure. But this was 1992, the same year that Peter Lilley made his speech to the Tory Party Conference denouncing young girls who get themselves pregnant to jump the housing queue. A bit like saying all MPs get themselves elected to fiddle their expenses. Hostile and absurd, but that was the climate of the day, all single mothers were benefit scroungers and a threat to the not-so-cosy nuclear family.

Early one morning, when you were only about three weeks old, just shortly after Simone had left for work and taken Elliott to nursery, I was tidying up the debris in our very small, galley kitchen. Simone cooked and I cleaned, that was the deal. There was a loud knock on the door of the flat. Still in my dressing gown, having been up in the night, I looked a proper sight, complete with leaking breast milk down my front and a not very attractive bed head, I was reluctant to open the door. As I answered and tentatively opened the door, this woman thrust her foot in the door, pushed it open, flashed some ID too quickly for me to check and rushed down the hall shouting. I was totally taken aback and it took me a few seconds to come to my senses with my only thought being for your safety. Instead of mugging me, this woman just kept shouting at me. She was shouting, *'Where is he, where is he?'* as she marched up and down the hall looking in all the rooms. Only after a few minutes of her shouting did it become clear that this was a very early morning visit from the CSA, the Child Support Agency.

I was scared and affronted by her Gestapo tactics, as she continued to roar at me looking for some man to support my child. To her, I was just another statistic among the single parents of Hackney, undeserving of any state benefits. I was not a new mother with a new baby, half exhausted through lack of sleep. I did everything I could to quell my indignation and anger, as I stood there in my dressing gown. How bloody dare she? Standing there, shaking with fury, I rose to my best assertive self and gave her a lecture about not judging people, that I was a social worker, had paid my taxes, had a job to go to and that she had no right harassing new mothers and single parents first thing in the morning. How bloody dare she!

I threw her out and slammed the door behind her, furious and swearing at the Tory Government and their reactionary underhand means barging into mothers' homes like this, only a few weeks after having a baby. Besides which, in our case, she was on a fruitless search. But I wasn't about to divulge our circumstances to someone from the state who had my name on some list as yet another scrounging single parent. Whenever I hear politicians judging people or talking about single mothers, I remember that particular incident and my blood boils. Fortunately for us, at least, that was an isolated incident and I had greater resolve than ever to ensure that I provided everything for you to avoid being subjected to such venom in the future. Show me still to this day a politician mouthing off about single mothers and I'll show you a well deserved punch in the face.

You will find that officialdom finds it very difficult to deal with anything new or different. Simone and I talked about pooling our resources to try and buy somewhere together. We made an appointment to see the mortgage advisor at the Halifax and after struggling into the room with our two buggies we explained that we were both single parents with a part-time and full time salary and we wanted to know how much they would give us to buy a house if we pooled our resources. The man's face was a picture. It didn't get any better when we explained that while determined and full of ambition for our children, at present, we were both broke and would need a 100% mortgage. He showed us the door.

That summer of 1992 was very hot. I have memories of proudly pushing the pram around Clissold Park. By this time, all of the friends I had met in the NCT antenatal class had all had their babies. We would congregate in a café in Stoke Newington Church Street and proceed to engage in a mass breast feeding session, somehow always managing to have that café to ourselves! Breast feeding in trendy cafes, taking you and Elliott to the park, organising trips to Scotland and just being immensely happy for me characterise the first six months of motherhood. I was both proud and happy, and we were settling into a routine.

The financial struggles that I encountered in those early months were not shared by the other new mums I knew, as I had fallen in with a very middle class set of NCT North London new mums. I tried to keep up the best I could with the outings and coffee mornings, knowing that I had paid work to look forward to in the New Year. I do not envy anyone who is forced to bring children up on benefits long term as it demands such resilience and stamina, not recognised by those who have always had comfortable means. Having been so focused on getting pregnant (with all my resources exhausted by that journey), I now had to adjust to the new and unbelievable costs associated with a new baby. Even though I could always rely upon the support of my family, it was nevertheless a struggle to get by every day and to keep up with the expectations of peers.

Water awareness for babies comes to mind. Once all the babies had all their first jabs, we enrolled you for these very early swimming classes. It mostly involved dunking the babies quickly under the water and smiling happily as you emerged, completely surprised by the whole exercise. I remember the trainer telling one of the mums, *'Perhaps you shouldn't hold baby under for quite so long next time, dear.'* We also had regular coffee mornings in each other's houses or flats and shared the ups and downs of dealing with new babies. However, we did not share the same anxieties. To me, the other mums seemed rather obsessed and perplexed about things that didn't really seem to matter at all. I was still determined to enjoy motherhood and was doing my best at breast feeding and following the advice of all the books. As the babies grew older and moved on to solids, there seemed to be a very strict NCT mothers' code in relation to the feeding and watering of our offspring, with far too many conversations about pureeing vegetables for my liking. Our group of mums would gather together with our babies and a collection of little plastic containers of pureed mush would appear. The others were totally taken aback when I allowed a white chocolate button to pass your lips. You were busy sucking the fingers off me while the other mums looked at me full of shock as their babies dined out on pureed spinach. The other mums were all lovely, if a little judgmental. I was very much the Scottish single parent of our group with my own way of doing things. This included, by necessity, going back to work full time.

NCT mums

Too quickly, my six months with you were gone and I was making arrangements to start my new job and organise childcare. I worked out that, as I was not paying a mortgage or expensive rent, I could afford a full time nursery place for you in a very nice nursery nearby but it would still take half my salary. I was going to work for a trade union which prided itself on being women friendly, so I was hopeful that I would negotiate some assistance for childcare as I made all the arrangements to start work in January 1993.

Chapter 12

On my thirty-second birthday, I started my second career as a full-time trade union official in London. The initial salary was not great, by London standards at least, but it came with a car, and I had hoped that the union would assist with some of my childcare costs. As ever, I was a woman before my time. I asked in my first staff meeting about childcare payments for working mothers. To a man, my colleagues, male trade union officials looked at me aghast. *'Childcare ? What do you mean? Are you having a laugh? We negotiate bigger and better cars, love.'* I exaggerate, I admit, but only slightly.

It soon became clear that I would not receive a penny, not a brass farthing, from a union which prided itself upon raising the rights of women workers with other employers. *Fan-bloody-tastic.* Childcare then was not even on their radar, never mind their bargaining agenda with other employers. This women friendly union was not so friendly to its female employees with childcare costs, and this was still the era of the Tory government, before childcare provisions and tax credits. Most of the other female officials in the union, and certainly those in senior positions, did not have children, having had to make the choice of career or motherhood. While it was an intellectual or political issue for them, it was hardly a pressing day to day problem. But for me, starting work and arranging childcare was cripplingly expensive. While the union prided itself upon being progressive enough to appoint a woman and a single parent to boot, there I was working full time but seriously broke. This brought an abrupt and painful realisation that this was to be my way of life for the foreseeable future. There would be no slack and money was a constant worry.

However, after a difficult few months, I resolved not to let the financial pressures of single parenthood, bills and childcare costs get me down. I decided to adopt my bank manager as my virtual partner and made acquaintance with a lifelong overdraft and very many flexible friends. I also decided not to remain silent in those endless meetings discussing bloody cars. Within the union hierarchy, status was reflected in the model and type of car you could negotiate, with standard issue for those of us on the bottom rung being a Ford Escort. I found this a bit too big for my needs and difficult to park in tight spaces at the TUC in Great Russell Street. Sensibly, I made some calls and agreed to take a smaller and cheaper Ford Fiesta instead. Common sense I thought, better for me and will save the union and its members money. But what seemed logical to me did not make me popular with many longstanding trade union officials. They did not want some new upstart woman (who ranted on all the time about childcare) undermining their rights to bigger company cars. I was, as they saw it, single handedly undermining years of proletariat struggle. This issue of company cars became such a bone of contention I threatened to stand for a position in the staff association on a platform of 'Nissan Micras for all'. I recall the absurdity of one well known official, the most vociferous about the union car issue, going on for hours about his right to a company car, even though he travelled to work on his bike as he preferred to cycle around London while the wife used the car. Madness. The importance of company cars to mostly male trade union officials, who failed to stop and consider the needs of working women, quickly opened my eyes to the old fashioned patriarchal approach of some trade unionists. It also explained how women's issues like childcare repeatedly fell off (or never made it onto) the negotiating agenda with employers.

My insistence that we must negotiate on childcare, maternity rights and flexible working led to ridicule and derision from hard-nosed negotiators who might just faint at the sight of a dirty nappy. I was not alone in trying to raise these issues. There were other women who had struggled to get to senior positions within the union movement. They had fought hard to get where they were. Part of their struggle had been to sacrifice having children so that they could compete on a level playing field with the men. But they never did. They still had to put up with misogyny and sexism. I remember one well known General Secretary meeting up with a group of senior female officials and demanding a kiss on the cheek. I respected some of these women but wondered how on earth they put up with that sort of behaviour. Although committed and determined, some female officials argued for feminist causes, like childcare, from an intellectual or political commitment, not from any real life experience. And so they would trawl off to evening meetings, breakfast meetings and weekend conferences without any understanding of the complicated arrangements working mothers had to make or costs of childcare. Unless you live with the reality, you cannot really understand the daily tensions and pressures of being a working mother.

I took you to the last ever NUPE conference at Scarborough in 1993. I rented a very small holiday flat. Your Nana came down to look after you for part of the week and then Linda came down for the rest of the time. Married but not yet a mother herself, she arrived with a large paperback book and was putting it into your changing bag. I asked when she exactly thought she would find time to read, and she said she was taking you to the beach for the day. Good luck with that idea, I thought. When I arrived back after the conference, she was traumatised by the stress of changing your nappy in Debenhams. She had tried to change you, but had used too much cream so that the new nappy wouldn't stick. She had to admit defeat and asked the woman in Debenhams if she had any Sellotape. They proceeded to secure the nappy with rounds and rounds of Sellotape while you remained blissfully happy amidst all the commotion. Later as a mother of three, including a set of twins, Linda operated with military precision and organisation.

When you were a baby, despite the constant financial pressures and the challenge of my new job, we managed to establish a routine of sorts. I approached the balancing act of motherhood and work very assertively as, after all, I had been so hugely pregnant at the interview, I reassured myself that they knew exactly what they were getting. Comment had been passed about how radical the union was for employing a single parent with a new baby with lots of self-congratulatory back slapping about being such a progressive organisation. This was my first (but far from last) experience of being conveniently adopted as an equal opportunities mascot and politically correct window dressing. I might have been allowed into the room to sit at the table, but no one else had any idea of the mammoth task it took just to arrive at work dressed and on time, never mind getting through each day. In the circumstances, however, I made no apology for leaving to collect you or putting you first in my life. I would face down any hint of criticism from some mediocre men who stayed around the office but achieved very little. I survived as a working mother and single parent by developing a very thick skin and facing down my detractors with a sharp retort or two. It required stamina and resilience, but I felt so lucky having you that all the effort was worthwhile and all my attention was focused on providing for you. If I arrived home feeling wound up after a bad day, irritated by the daily frustrations of dealing with clueless judgmental colleagues or petty union politics it only took a few hours with you, to settle my nerves and lift my spirits so that I could face it all again the next day. I loved our evenings and weekends together, bath times and endless story telling, spending hours at the park and seeing you thrive at nursery. When you were asleep, I would look at you in your cot and any doubts about whether I could manage would disappear. I had no other option. I was your mother, first and foremost, and it was entirely down to me to provide you with the best future I could.

Around this same time, as I was establishing our new routine and things were falling into place, Simone somehow managed to find some money or used her credit card to organise a holiday to Brazil to visit a friend who lived there. She went with Elliott for a three week holiday, only to arrive back a few weeks later with a new man in her life. Very shortly after that holiday, and without much discussion, he moved into the flat. Surprised and frankly rather pissed off that we had had no discussion as to how this would impact upon our living situation in a very small flat, I moved out and quickly rented a stupidly expensive house near your nursery, ironically called Independent Place.

This had not been part of *any* plan. From the outside, all looked fine. I was working full-time, you were at a good nursery, we had a car and a nice place to live. We got by, but I was massively broke all the time, living in London in permanent overdraft and resigned to debt. I managed to keep the wolf from the Fox's door, only by constantly robbing Peter to pay Paul. Again, I had to rely on my increased overdraft and I moved to the land of the minimum monthly payment. For me, juggling finances to pay everything from one salary rather than two has been the greatest challenge of single parenthood. It is a constant pressure, and it can be very difficult and demoralising. But it comes with the territory of motherhood and single parenthood in particular. Since the early morning Gestapo raid of the CSA, I would rather be proudly and hugely indebted. I focused solely on your needs in the short term, in the hope that in the longer term if I worked hard, when retirement arrived some kind soul would buy a toothless old lady a bag of chips. Adopting the philosophy of good debt (*education, houses, books, travel*) and bad debt (*shoes, overpriced cappuccinos, clothes you don't wear*), I resigned myself to a never ending monthly challenge.

Those early years in London were a financial nightmare, with constant financial pressures, but I kept telling myself it was all good debt associated with the essentials of bringing up my child, my longed for child, who would want for nothing. I would push your buggy along Stoke Newington's Church Street walking past all the shops with expensive candles, earrings, vases or delicatessens with over-priced cheese. Some people spent more on smelly cheese each week than other families received in benefits. Then, I knew that I couldn't afford to buy nice things, but I made a pact that one day I would be able to go in to each shop along the length of Church Street and buy myself a small present, but for the moment I concentrated on you. As long as I could give you what you needed, that was all I cared about, and of course your Nana and Papa were always there to help.

Occasionally, if Simone could babysit, I would go out in the evening with the other mums, either to a bar or sometimes to their houses. We were a diverse group, from one mum who had a husband and a lovely house with bottle green radiators painted to match the walls, to me - the single parent living in a council block in Hackney. But they all had partners. All of our babies were around the same age and it was good to talk about our different experiences. I found it amusing listening to them, trying to keep up with each other and the endless complaints and frustrations that their partners were not supportive, not doing enough around the house and generally being a waste of space. These tales of woe would go on for ages, but when there was a lull in the conversation they would all turn to me and wonder how I possibly managed as a single parent, '*That must be so hard*'. My response was that, apart from being broke all the time, I didn't have to put up with all the shit they had been discussing for the past hour. They were aghast at the idea that any aspect of being a single parent might be an improvement on their situations, even though the matching radiators and the husband were not apparently guaranteeing domestic bliss. Oh no, despite it all they said they could never manage on their own. As I finished my coffee, I tried as politely as possible to point out that they hadn't even tried to manage on their own, and that statistically speaking a few of the group might just become single parents in the future. For me, there were definitely benefits of not being in a conventional situation and I certainly did not want anyone feeling sorry for us, or for you. I was not full of angst about whether I should work full or part-time as I did not have that luxury, nor did I join in the endless hand wringing or talk of guilt. That just seemed such a pointless waste of my precious time.

At the same time, I was living on the crest of an emotional wave, feeling empowered and relieved that I had finally achieved motherhood. Life was challenging with a new baby and a new job in London, within a year. I was assertive, dealing with the demands of work and besides, as I constantly reminded myself, as I fell down exhausted at the end of every week, I was invincible.

In June 1993, we organised a big party to mark your first birthday, and Mum and Dad came down from Scotland. Around the same time, there was also a huge party at the Esperance Hospital to celebrate all the babies born through assisted conception. We took the train down as I had done many times before from London Victoria to Eastbourne, but this time you were beside me asleep in your buggy. At the party, one of the nurses had dressed up as a giant bunny and you howled as soon as she came near you, but otherwise it was a great day, with lots of happy people celebrating being parents against the odds.

As motherhood had been my choice, I was determinedly upbeat and also found reserves of energy to keep going when I just wanted to fall down. I lost weight and I tried to keep up appearances, dying my increasingly grey hair. Outwardly, I was the epitome of a trendy London middle class mother. In your first year, I have a picture of us at a baby massage class. I am a size ten, my hair is a strange mixture, orangey blonde on top and black down the sides and at the back. I look fantastic and I am carefully massaging my baby on the floor and you are smiling and happy. You can't capture those moments in words. All seemed right with the world of you and me, and nothing else mattered.

Nana was by now a long distance commuting granny. She made regular trips to London about every six weeks on her nights off from the hospital, often sleeping on the train to

London after a row of eight back to back night shifts, so that she could spend her days off with us in London. No account of those early days would be complete without recognising the support given to me by Nana and by Simone. Despite us moving out of her flat, we lived close enough around the corner that we still helped each other out with childcare and I tried to see Elliott as much as I could.

During my time with NUPE and Unison, I even worked in Belfast for a month Monday to Friday. I had to arrange an army of friends and family to provide backup childcare and to stay with you during the week. It was really hard but it was possible – just. Even so, few of the officials in the union, who espoused equal opportunities in theory, had any idea of the effort it took to organise a working month away from home and the sacrifice it entailed. Frankly, they did not have a clue, and this underlined for me again the chasm that exists between people who blithely talk about the ideal of equality and those who live it, through the daily struggles, to secure even a small piece of the action. Nevertheless, I was keen to make a good impression in my new job and was, as ever, ambitious wanting to do well in my new career to give you a good life.

Although I was permanently overdrawn, I recognised that I needed to buy somewhere to live rather than continue to pay expensive rent. I managed against all the odds to buy a house. This was not so much a sub-prime as a completely brass-neck mortgage, underpinned by the determination to keep forging ahead. We moved into our new Barratt house two days before Christmas 1993. With the house and mortgage, caring for you and meeting childcare costs and the demanding full-time union official job, it became much harder to convince myself that I was invincible. The reality was that I was frequently completely exhausted, and permanently broke. But I was utterly determined not to show that face to the world. Outwardly, I tried to be as upbeat as possible.

The worst memory I have, is when as a toddler you fell

down at nursery and I had to take you to hospital. I had come to collect you after work as normal and the nursery staff said you had just fallen over in the garden for no apparent reason, as if you had fainted. They were a bit worried but hadn't called me at work. By this time it was too late to go to the GP, so I drove you to St Elizabeth's Children's Hospital. They kept you in overnight for observation and although I had come straight from work, no one came near me or even offered me a cup of tea. I didn't want to leave you, so I sat by your bed all night worried sick. That night, I admit I wished there was someone there to put their arms around me and tell me everything would be okay. I couldn't bear the idea that there might be something wrong with you. It was a long night. When you were discharged the next day, they referred you to Great Ormond Street for further tests. When we went for the appointment a few weeks later, the doctor wanted to do some brain scans and covered your head with electrodes. You thought it was a funny game, but I wanted to be sick. My insides were churning and I could not rest until all the results came back without any problems. Apart from that, you were quite healthy with recurring ear infections being the most frequent reason to see the GP.

As life settled into a routine and you were becoming a toddler, I started to wonder about more fertility treatment. The possibility of a second baby had not entered my head before, as I had been so focused on getting pregnant just once, if at all possible. But now I had you, this wonderful little person toddling around, chatting away and bringing me such joy, it seemed only natural to want to try again. I desperately wanted to give you a brother or sister and wanted the experience of motherhood once more if I could.

Around this time, Simone had decided to emigrate to Canada where her father lived. So Elliott when he was four had moved with Simone to live in Vancouver. He was my godson and having been so involved in his early life, I missed him and I tried my best to keep in touch.

111

Thoughts of another baby kept popping into my head at the most unexpected times. In the middle of a union meeting or driving through the Blackwall tunnel I would, all of a sudden, be distracted by thoughts of babies. Yet, there we were settled in London, just about managing to get by on our own and you were happy and well. It was just crazy to think that I could have more than this. Keeping busy, I kept trying to put these thoughts out of my head. I thought long and hard. Part of me knew it was madness, but another part of me thought it seemed to be a perfectly natural reaction to want to try to be a mother again. Eventually, I very tentatively broached the subject.

I was not fully prepared for the reaction of my nearest and dearest. Friends and family thought I was completely mad. There was a shocked reaction from all who remembered (perhaps more than me) the misery of the twelve fertility cycles which had finally resulted in one wonderful pregnancy. Of course, I thought a great deal about asking for too much from life. But being content with my lot was just not in my nature. I tried to persuade myself that I should try to make the most of what I had. But it nagged at me. I did listen to the serious doubts of family and friends, who could just not contemplate, nor understand why I would put myself through it all again. Having a baby was by far the most powerful thing I had ever achieved in my life. That feeling of watching you safely asleep in your cot at night was beyond words.

I was endlessly surprised by an overwhelming feeling of joy, that you were actually mine and these waves of happiness overtook me at the most unexpected times. They still do. I loved the walk home from nursery, holding your hand, while you giggled or chatted away about your day or at the park at the weekend playing on the swings, trips to the Early Learning Centre with a bright child eager to learn, even endless evenings playing with the little people in the Duplo house (putting them to bed and getting them all up again a few seconds later which could go on for hours before bedtime). Mothers are not often encouraged to dwell on, or share the joys and delights of motherhood. Instead, the magazines and newspapers are all about the stress and the never ending *guilt*. Guilt? About what, exactly? I could never understand. I was not in the least guilty about anything.

Natasha (furthest left) at Nursery

Of course it wasn't all divine, when you wouldn't sleep or when toddler tantrums arrived, but we got through the day, and most of the time you were a lively and happy wee girl. Even at nursery you were a lively little character organising all the other kids. BBC2 came to the nursery to make a documentary about gender stereotyping and I had to sign a release to say you could take part. There was a hilarious bit where you walked right up to the camera and asked what they were doing. Bright as a button, you recognised all the clothes from the other children in the nursery, so the staff would take you into the laundry room and hold up all the clothes with missing labels as they came out of the dryer, and you could tell them who owned the unidentified clothes. You were a wee chatterbox too, asking endless questions and making up stories.

Your Nana did give me a hard time for spending so much

time and money at the Early Learning Centre. In her day, mothers did not get to spend the same fun times with their kids. One day when she was visiting us in London, she wondered aloud how she had managed with two children under two and a job as a night nurse. Without undermining her efforts, I gently tried to remind her that in the early sixties she would strap us both into the high pram with a hot water bottle and park us at the end of the garden while she got on with her dusting. Motherhood was different then. I wasn't at all sure that I could manage with two children, but I was convinced that I could be a mother again if I was determined enough. I could indeed do it again and I would manage somehow.

So I called Dr. Robertson.

At Eastbourne with Dr. Robertson.

He perfectly understood why I wanted to try for another baby but said I needed some more tests first.

On 12th September 1994, when you were two years and four months, I went through the most excruciating procedure known to womankind, nothing short of gynaecological torture, called a *Hyster-o-salp-ingo-gram*. In this procedure, dye is forced up inside you to see if the reproductive pathway is clear or if there are any worrying blockages. It was awful, truly awful and the bad news was that the test came back completely negative, stating that my remaining anatomy of one tube and one ovary were blocked and frankly knackered.

Devastated, I refused to believe this news and arranged a further operation in October 1994. I underwent a further laparoscopy at the Esperance Hospital in Eastbourne. The news after that operation was much better. My remaining ovary and tube looked okay. Strange, how different doctors can give you completely different results. So all was set for me to begin fertility treatment again early in 1995, but sadly not with the same donor.

Chapter 13

On the 6th February 1995, I started fertility cycle number thirteen, taking the prescribed drugs and injections, and went into hospital to have GIFT, which at that time was thought to be more successful than IVF, as conception was encouraged to take place in the body rather than a test tube. In this cycle, three eggs were transferred and I secretly lived in the mad hope of healthy triplets. But I was also prepared for another long fertility journey, and so was therefore not too despondent when that cycle failed. Fortunately, that cycle had also produced six frozen embryos and so with a short wait, I had IVF on cycle number fourteen on 3rd March 1995, when another three frozen embryos were thawed and transferred.

As part of the treatment, you are invited to view your embryos down the microscope pre-transfer. This made the lack of pregnancy all the more tragic, because conception had happened but the embryos then failed to implant. From then on, I never wanted to look at my potential children, a few cells old, dividing under a microscope. Anyone who goes through infertility treatment has to put great faith in doctors and in science. But the emotional roller coaster is overwhelming and it can be difficult to hold on during the rollercoaster ride. There is always the feeling that you might just go over the side. Sometimes too, all the scientific theory and medical rituals just do not translate into a pregnancy for no apparent reason. No matter how posh the hospital, and no matter how good the doctors, sometimes it is just not to be. Ironically, as my dates worked out I was in hospital for cycle number fifteen on 2nd June 1995 – your third birthday, when a further three embryos were transferred. Sadly, these babies did not happen either.

Despite these disappointments, I gave my body a few months rest and had to gather together further financial resources before I could attempt cycle number sixteen in March 1996.

I remember sitting in the waiting room of the hospital in Eastbourne when the BBC broke news of the Dunblane massacre in Scotland on 13th March 1996. It was hard to believe what was unfolding before our eyes in a quiet Scottish village. I wondered what type of world I was bringing another child into, and wanted to rush home to make sure you were safe, even though you were with your Nana.

Despite their reservations, your grandparents continued to help me as much as they could. A further GIFT cycle resulted in three eggs transferred, but this cycle was again unsuccessful with no reason for the continued failure. In April 1996 and cycle number seventeen, I had three frozen embryos transferred but was once again not pregnant by the end of yet another round of fertility treatment. By this stage, I was very despondent and extremely disappointed, as even the most high tech and expensive fertility treatment seemed as though it was not going to work. You were nearly four and my focus had to be on you starting school. I then seriously wondered if we should stay in London or move back to Scotland.

After much thought, I made the very difficult but conscious decision to stop fertility treatment to concentrate on your welfare. I also decided that we should move back to Scotland to be near the family we did have, before you started primary school. Simone and Elliott were by that time settled in Canada and it seemed a very sensible move, especially for you, although I still had some serious reservations about bringing you up in Scotland. I wanted to avoid the narrow expectations and prejudices I had experienced, and wanted you to live in a positive community where the world was full of possibilities.

The first step was to request a transfer via the union to a position in Scotland, but nothing happened. I waited, not so patiently, and lobbied the relevant decision makers within the union every week. I was covering a large patch in London and some other officers were off sick, so my transfer request was not top priority. Finally, demoralised by the internal politics of the union, I began to apply for other jobs back in Scotland. I then arranged to move back to Scotland and stay temporarily with Nana and Papa in Motherwell, while I rented out the house in London. I had an interview for a national position with another union in Scotland and was very much focused on moving back north and putting the disappointments of cycle number seventeen behind me.

Despite it all, I was making every effort to move into the next chapter of our lives, returning to Scotland as positively as possible.

Then there was a very peculiar twist of fate. In the very same week, I received two official letters with different opportunities. In the space of a few days, I had the official letter offering me my new job in Glasgow as the Scottish official of a small union. I accepted the job immediately. The very next day, I had a letter from Eastbourne. This letter told me that they had located further vials of the same donor that had worked with you and they wanted me to know in case I wanted to try again. I was elated but very confused.

We were in the middle of a move back to Scotland. Shit – I thought - should we go back north as planned or stay in London? After much thought, I decided to move back to Scotland for your sake. But I also bought up *all* supplies of our previously lucky donor and banked it for future use.

Then I quickly arranged one cycle of IUI with super drugs and this great sperm in October 1996. This was in the same year where there had been tragic media frenzy over Mandy Allwood who had conceived eight babies, all of whom had died. It so happened that during this eighteenth cycle, my one remaining ovary super ovulated and produced fourteen eggs in one cycle. Dr. Robertson gave me a very stern talking to about the risks of proceeding with that cycle of treatment, but we both thought that with my history we could take the risk and not lose the opportunity of so many eggs. I worried myself sick for two weeks that I might be like the old woman who lived in

118

the shoe with too many children she didn't know what to do. And yet after an agonising two weeks not one, not one of those bloody fourteen eggs, had implanted and I was not pregnant again. How is that bloody possible, I ask you? I couldn't bear that it wasn't working again, even though all seemed to go well during the cycles themselves. It looked like I would just need to keep going for twelve more cycles as before.

I was hooked once again. Each successive failed fertility treatment only made me more determined to keep going, as I weighed up the statistics and convinced myself that the next roll of the dice or mega injection of super drugs would do the trick. I might have been on the train north with my one child and my sad and disappointing ovary, but I was also well and truly back on the rollercoaster of fertility treatment. What if I try just one more time?

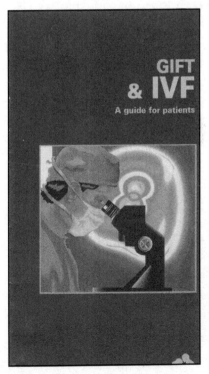

Chapter 14

The move back from London to Lanarkshire in the west coast of Scotland was a huge challenge. To me, it felt like going back in time. I felt apprehensive about moving back to Scotland, but I was clear that I was making the right choice for you. I wanted you to be settled before you started school. Although my job was in Glasgow, I was determined to bring you up in Edinburgh, to avoid all the west coast sectarian banalities of my own childhood. I wanted you to thrive in an atmosphere where the world was your oyster and life was full of possibilities. The Scottish psyche is not renowned for its optimism and self-confidence, so I knew that it would be my job to carve out a protective niche for our alternative single parent family. I had left Scotland with the reactionary views of the medical profession ringing in my ears. Nevertheless, I was optimistic that I was now thick skinned enough to survive back in Scotland.

At first, we lived in Motherwell for nine months when we moved back while I was looking for a house in Edinburgh. You went to a lovely wee Montessori nursery in Bothwell and your Nana and Papa collected you while I was at work. While you were there, you played Mary in the Christmas nativity play and your Nana managed to find some blue cloth to make a costume.

Tasha as Mary

It makes me laugh – given my profound difficulty with organised religion – that you now have your photograph, as the Holy Mary aged four, as one of your profile pictures on Facebook, but it would make your great grandmother very happy indeed.

While we were back in Motherwell, you made friends with the girl across the road. Heather was a few years older and came to visit us for a weekend when we finally moved to Edinburgh. She was very quiet in the back of the car, as we drove towards the M8 then this small voice piped up asking, '*Carol, do they use the same money in Edinburgh?*'. Yes, I reassured her, folk in Edinburgh just live an hour away in the car, in the same country, so they use the same money. She seemed a bit reassured, but was still quite quiet and looked a bit worried as I watched her face through the rear view mirror. Then after a few more silent minutes, she gathered her courage and said in a louder voice, '*Carol, is it true that you've never had a husband?*' I smiled as we drove away from Motherwell towards Edinburgh and said, '*Yes, that's true, but it is a very long story, maybe you should talk to your mum about it.*'

We had arranged to move to Edinburgh in time for you to start school in August 1997. All my careful plans went hellishly wrong as our new build part-exchange Barratt house was far from completion. After a short stint renting a flat in Bruntsfield, we ended up in bed and breakfast accommodation. I had threatened to sue Barratt and go to the papers if they didn't sort out temporary accommodation. Worse still, my friend Barbara who was a teacher in Germany had arranged for one of her pupils, Tanya, to come to do a gap year in Edinburgh, to learn English and to be our *au pair.* That year the best laid plans of my invincible self resulted in us all living in temporary bed and breakfast accommodation, including our German *au pair*. I even had to stand my ground to ensure that we were not all in the same family room. What a nightmare. Despite all my best efforts, those first few weeks at primary school were terrible. You cried and protested that you did not

121

like being in the bed and breakfast and you did not want an *au pair*, you wanted to move back to London or to Nana's. As I left you in the playground lining up with the other children, I asked the teacher to keep an eye on you. When Mrs. Laurie asked me what was wrong I burst into floods of tears in front of a class full of five year olds! Mortified, I gave her a plant with a note of apology at home time.

Once we moved into the house and you had settled at school, life was much easier. Although you quickly found out that your new school friends went to something called 'After School Club' which sounded lots of fun. One afternoon you had a mega tantrum when Tanya came to collect you from school, because you wanted to go to the club instead and you told her that you hated *au pairs*. You scared the living daylights out of her and I arrived home from work later to find the pair of you in tears. So it ended up that I was even more broke than usual that whole year, as I paid for both the *au pair* and the After School Club. Tanya was supposed to do some housework in exchange, but she was not great at cleaning and was more interested in learning English and going out. Unexpectedly, I had also acquired a teenager. Meanwhile, you thrived at school and loved all the activities at after school club and eventually everything settled down. With you finally settled and past your fifth birthday, I was seriously wondering about more fertility treatment, after all time was pressing, as I was now thirty-six.

But how was I going to manage further treatment in Eastbourne, now that I was based back in Scotland? Could I get treatment in Scotland? Surely, I thought attitudes might have changed in ten years? I hoped that things just might be different and optimistically wrote to private fertility clinics in Edinburgh and Glasgow. I had absolutely no expectation that I could get any treatment on the NHS. Although I had been a higher rate tax payer and worked constantly, I knew that it was a battle too far to take on the state and expect fair and equal treatment from the NHS. Besides, I did not have the time to try as my one remaining ovary was ageing by the day. I wrote to three doctors, let's just call them X, Y and Z in Edinburgh and Glasgow and received identical answers. The familiar outraged NO WAY. So I made plans to resume treatment in Eastbourne while somehow commuting from Edinburgh.

Telling you that now, it does seem just a little bit crazy, but by that time I was once again gripped by the possibility of managing to get pregnant again. I was determined to overcome all practical problems, money, travelling hundreds of miles for treatment, somehow it would all work out. I just had to be determined enough.

As a single parent working full time, I would wake up every morning looking very far removed from the image of an invincible feminist. I gravitated towards strong black coffee and held on to the conviction that my stamina and determination would see me through the hurdles to come. I became quite adept at worrying in a chronological fashion, lining all the obstacles up in date order and deciding which needed to be tackled first. Being a trade union official and working with some very traditional Scottish teachers in a small and then fairly right wing trade union remained a daily grind and was at times far from an uplifting experience. Since moving back to Edinburgh on the eve of the Scottish Parliament Referendum, I had transferred my Labour Party membership and was also once again immersed in local politics.

In order of priority, I was first and foremost your mother, a single parent and you always came first. This was not then and sadly is not even now, the received wisdom in most workplaces. I tried to make sure that I organised myself to ensure that my professional responsibilities came a very close second. As I was working in a hostile environment with lots of internal politics, I did not want to give my detractors ready ammunition to use against me. The Ginger Rodgers quote about *"Having to do everything men do only better and backwards while wearing high heels,"* comes to mind. No matter how hard I worked, I faced difficulties and criticisms from certain quarters, particularly from those that had failed to get my job. There was a storm brewing.

In my experience, the reality of working mothers helping each other out, taking kids to and from school and helping with babysitting for late meetings and shifts was the only way we managed to get through the day and cope with the different demands. You must remember when our neighbours split up? For Kate, a midwife with early shifts starting at 7 am, getting to work became a huge problem. We would help each other when we could, I would take all you kids to school and Kate would pick you all up. I still recall the sight of her two wee girls on my door step at 6:30 am, still in their pyjamas with their little individual packs of their favourite cereal in hand. Mothers especially make herculean efforts just to get themselves to work, to the hospital or office which are almost always unrecognised.

Looking back at that time my drive and determination to achieve certain goals seemed perfectly logical life choices, at least for a hyperactive malcontent feminist. And so with you settled at school, living in Edinburgh in our new house, managing work demands and finally qualifying for paid maternity leave my life was organised and secure enough to welcome another baby.

I flew from Edinburgh to the South Coast of England to resume fertility treatment and attempt number nineteen in January 1998. The logistics dictated by the drug regime, the injections and the required scans of my remaining ovary were impossible to manage over such a long distance. Despite the Scottish medical opposition and the impossibility of securing fertility treatment in the country of my birth, it transpired that Dr. Robertson still had some influence north of the border. On my behalf, he persuaded Dr. C to undertake the required scans during the crucial periods of treatment to make sure the treatment was conducted safely and I was closely monitored. This is how my path came to cross again with the very same doctor who advised in the strongest possible terms that I should not dare to think of having a child "out of wedlock". If I had listened to him and been constrained by that advice, my whole life would have taken a different path and you would not be here.

Yet, here I was wantonly turning up in his clinic nearly a decade later, as a single mother to a five year old, and with my half-life ovary, eager to become pregnant again. Without looking at my notes and without the intervention of Dr. Robertson, this Godlike consultant, who bestowed the gift of life and changed the destiny of women, would not even have remembered my name. But fortunately for me, he was willing to do a favour for an old friend and medical colleague.

Cycle nineteen in January 1998 therefore involved complicated trips from Edinburgh to the south of England and to the west of Scotland and was sadly unsuccessful. During what was supposed to be another routine scan in the clinic in Monklands Hospital, Dr. C looked very serious. He then told me that I could not go ahead with further treatment, as I had developed yet another ovarian cyst.

I really thought he must be bloody joking. What the hell? A third cyst on an ovary removed twice already?

He advised me to see my GP as soon as possible. This was not only devastating news, it was verging on the surreal. According to the scans, the same ovary that had developed the two previous cysts and been removed twice, had re-grown and developed a third cyst. This was just *un-bloody-believable.* Somehow, I had become a mutating bionic women, cloning and re-growing malfunctioning reproductive organs, while paying shedloads of money for private fertility treatment. You just couldn't make it up. Life is much stranger than fiction.

Frustrated and angry, I had little idea where my fertility journey would take me next. I remember sitting in the car park of Monklands hospital trying to take in the news that I had a

125

third ovarian cyst. I had been advised to see my GP straight away, so I called and made an urgent appointment.

I found myself once again a patient in a gynaecology ward, this time in the Edinburgh Royal Infirmary. I had gone to my GP with the evidence from the scan and was immediately referred to the hospital. No one can yet explain to me how the same ovary managed to re-grow twice and malfunction three times. By this stage in my career as a gynae patient, I had almost an encyclopaedic knowledge of the female anatomy. I understood that somehow my internal plumbing was not complying with the expected order of things. But by this stage, I no longer blamed my feminist politics, my failed Catholicism nor my discontented nature, as there seemed to be some medical phenomenon beyond all understanding. The doctors just shook their heads when I asked for answers to my exploding organs.

With all further fertility treatment put on hold, I was discharged from hospital in Edinburgh after my third major operation and was advised to see the consultant at the follow up appointment in six weeks. I duly attended the outpatients department and as I sat in there in yet another hospital waiting room to see this female doctor, Dr. W, I noticed a poster on the wall for the Edinburgh Assisted Conception Unit. Ironically it seemed, while I qualified for life saving NHS treatment to avoid the risk of yet another growing and bursting ovarian cyst, I could only be a patient in one respect. Crucially, they could get me back in working order but I was not then allowed to be a patient of the fertility clinic. When I was discharged, and advised that my one ovary was still working and intact, I wrote to this female consultant, pouring out my whole story and pointing out the unacceptable hypocrisy of being allowed access to limited medical treatment which had sorted out my errant re-growing reproductive organs but highlighting that the very same doctors could not countenance that I would want to put my remaining organ to some good and proper use, to become a mother again while it remained possible.

126

My letter to Dr. W. must have caused much internal discussion, as I was then given an appointment on 25th June 1998 at the Assisted Conception Unit at the Edinburgh Royal Infirmary. I was then, to my absolute amazement, accepted for fertility treatment in Edinburgh. Their one condition was that I had to agree to counselling to see if I was fit to become a parent and to allow them to assess the welfare of the child. By that stage, I was more than willing to agree to all and any conditions, no matter how absurd. While making the appointment with the counsellor to see if I would make a fit parent, I did point out that I was already a single parent of six year old!

Nevertheless, I was ecstatic. Finally, I was going to get treatment in Scotland. It would still be privately funded with no help from the NHS, but the logistics of treatment at home were so much simpler. It had taken over a decade, but I was to be accepted for fertility treatment in Scotland, as far as I knew the first ever single woman to be allowed fertility treatment north of the border.

Indeed, a seismic shift in Scottish gender politics. It felt wonderful that I had reached a very significant watershed in my fertility battles and I was convinced that this meant that good things lay ahead, if only I remained determined and did not give up. After all, before you were born, when I had left for London and the unknown reproductive battles ahead, I had no permanent job, no home and no security. A decade later, I was settled back in Edinburgh, I was working full-time, qualified for paid maternity leave, and had a big sister and a supportive family waiting for this next baby. Sorted.

I contacted the clinic in Eastbourne and arranged for the remaining sperm stored there to be transported to Scotland. This transfer involved further expense of a few hundred pounds and was not entirely straight forward as they had some problems finding the hospital. A few urgent phone calls to my mobile and directions over the phone to the hospital finally ensured safe delivery of this very precious cargo.

All was in place. With great excitement, I started cycle number twenty in Scotland. I was not only conscious of being the first single woman in Scotland to access fertility treatment, I also felt very keenly that the hospital and doctors had taken a risk on me, my aging errant ovary and my complicated medical history. Unfortunately, as is the way with matters of great import and excitement, it proved to be a crushing disappointment. During that first Scottish cycle, for some reason the fertility drugs failed to stimulate enough follicles and IVF had to be abandoned. In order not to waste my eggs and the vial of defrosted super sperm, we agreed on a last ditch attempt at IUI but to no avail. After all that fanfare, it was the same sad and disappointing outcome.

In the midst of all this, I had been successful in another respect. The Scottish Referendum had been a success in 1997 and the wheels were quickly put in motion for the first Scottish Parliament elections in May 1999. Knowing that all the best seats would have been carved up long ago, I nevertheless decided to apply to be a Labour Party candidate. This involved a very new Labour process of filling out an application form and, if short listed, being called to interview to be vetted by an interview panel of the great and the good in the Scottish Labour Party. It proved to be a hugely controversial process, as very many able and dedicated Labour activists (and indeed some sitting councillors and MPs) were deemed not good enough to stand for the new Scottish Parliament. Crazy and some now assess the beginning of the demise of the Labour Party in Scotland. Very many of my friends, especially those with a history of feminist campaigning within the party, were rejected as potential candidates. The awkward squad was to be replaced by New Labour candidates who agreed to be obediently "on message".

As I had been away in London for such a long time, I was not well known enough, nor yet plugged into the right circles to ensure a safe seat. However on the positive side, having been in London for eight years, I had not been embroiled in bitter political battles within Scottish Labour and, as such, was not singled out as someone to be blocked at the interview stage. As one well known trade union official and stalwart of the party said to me, '*You're at the cow's tail, hen,*' and offered little hope that I would get through the approval process, to fight even an unwinnable seat. With nothing to lose and having overcome my own personal fertility battles, I decided to apply and was duly called for interview at Labour Party Headquarters in Glasgow.

As talking has always been my personal forte, I performed well enough at the interview. I answered questions honestly about my political views, membership of the party in Scotland and in London, my enthusiasm for the Scottish Parliament, the detail of party policies and the fact that I was naturally on the left of the party as both a socialist and a feminist. Besides which, almost everyone on the panel knew of the far left antics of my older brother Colin, so there was no point in trying to present myself as some New Labour clone, as that would in any event have been very far from the truth.

At the end of the interview, I was asked the one question put to all potential Parliamentary candidates. '*Is there anything in your life which might bring embarrassment to the party or anything else which you should disclose to the panel?*' My reply was unequivocal and very simple. I told them that I was far from embarrassed, but I was a single parent by choice, as a result of fertility treatment in London, that you were the greatest achievement of my life, and that as a candidate I would never ever be apologetic nor on the back foot about my life choices. I said very clearly that I would seek party approval *only* on that basis and that if it was a problem for them, then I should not be endorsed as a candidate. To my surprise, following the interview I was approved as a potential Scottish Labour Party candidate, but perhaps they gave approval safe in the knowledge that I had no hope of being elected.

This was merely the very first stage of a long process. It meant that I was endorsed as a potential candidate, but there were still many hurdles ahead in terms of getting selected to fight a seat or get onto the regional lists. I thought the experience of being a candidate would be invaluable, but I had no expectation whatsoever of being elected to the first Scottish Parliament. Obtaining this party approval was therefore for me something of a double edged sword. Very many of my friends were rejected, so it was with mixed feelings and some surprise that I looked ahead as a potential candidate for the first Scottish Parliament election in 1999. There was a big rally for all the approved candidates to meet Tony Blair and Donald Dewar. There was another event in Princes Street with Donald Dewar to unveil a new Labour Party poster and they wanted lots of children and asked candidates to bring their kids. But no one had thought to look after the children left waiting around and I remember having to buy lots of ice creams to keep all the children happy. Donald Dewar shook your hand and said you had the same cheeky face as your mother. Charming. I often wonder if that poster launch with pictures of you and the other children is in the news archives somewhere?

As I had anticipated, although no selection meetings had actually taken place, the whole thing had already been completely carved up. To ensure gender balance, all Scottish constituencies had been twinned to select one female and one male candidate. This led to the usual horse trading and deals being done to produce a double ticket of a male and female candidate. In reality, very few people in politics, male or female, are elected on merit. It is all about horse trading, who stays about longest to be in the right place at the right time, and a certain amount of luck. People who are against quotas for women argue that politicians should be elected on merit but they obviously have not met very many male, and sadly some female, politicians completely devoid of any merit but obedient and with friends in high places. The selection process then and now has much more to do with having the momentum and support of the party machine and learning to bite tongues to stay "on message". In Scotland, especially in safe seats, the Labour Party machine overplayed its hand and, with notable exceptions, produced a generation of safe and largely uninspiring candidates.

While I sent my CV around and attended a number of selection meetings, it was more for the experience than in any expectation of success. I was invited to attend selection meetings in Aberdeen and was nominated as one of only two female candidates. I took you with me to a few meetings and you sat at the back of the room being a cheeky monkey, making faces at me throughout my five minute speech. I won the final meeting but unfortunately for me the other local female candidate had mobilised the postal vote, she won the overall vote by a very narrow margin and then went on to be elected as the MSP. I was, however, very philosophical as I had not expected to get so close and being an MSP for a constituency in Aberdeen would have presented its own logistical problems.

I was then invited to stand for the completely unwinnable seat of Edinburgh West, where the competition would be less stiff as there was absolutely no prospect of Labour getting elected, ever. What an offer. Did I want to fight an unwinnable seat in my own time, at entirely my own expense in a vast constituency with only a handful of activists and volunteers? Hell, I thought, why not, it will be good experience. And so, I was selected to be the Scottish Labour Party Parliamentary candidate for Edinburgh West in 1999.

Meanwhile, my parallel life of drug taking and expensive fertility treatments continued and I was ever hopeful that all the omens were good, with treatment in Scotland and with the same donor this must mean something after all my battles and ups and downs.

I was convinced that cycle number twenty-one in January 1999 would be my lucky number. The whole process of being a private patient in the NHS hospital was a far cry from my previous treatments in Eastbourne. It felt more basic and routine, with only a curtain between patients rather than a private room, but I pushed any doubts to the back of my mind, just very grateful to have been accepted for treatment. This was surely it, at last?

Christmas in Aviemore

Natasha's first day at primary school

Chapter 15

In January 1999, I commenced cycle twenty-one of fertility treatment. This cycle of IVF in Edinburgh went well, and three embryos were transferred. I was utterly convinced that I would find myself pregnant again and even engaged in delirious window shopping for double and even triple buggies. There is no way truly to explain the fervour of fertility treatment and the whole rollercoaster of emotions which grip your very being, making you feel fantastically powerful and wholly devastated within half a menstrual cycle. All the statistical odds mess with your emotions and your head. And for me it had worked once before after twelve attempts, so I just had to remain powerful and determined. It was just a matter of keeping going. But alas, once again it was not to be and the two week painful wait ended again in disappointment. I was once again let down with another thud.

Meanwhile, the other political aspects of my life took a turn from the sublime to the ridiculous. Just after this further failed cycle, I found myself attending a Burns Supper later that same month. It was an old fashioned and formal affair, kilts and speeches, haggis and whisky. I was seated at the top table. I was introduced to a journalist and his partner, who happened to be a midwife. To make the dull evening more bearable as the speeches and Burns poems droned on in the background, I talked to this midwife about matters reproductive and babies. She was very nice, understanding and a good listener and I shared a truncated version of my reproductive battles, ending with a not to be defeated flourish that I had you, and I was the first single woman in Scotland to gain access to fertility treatment. So there, full of bravado, I told her that I was determined to try again and she wished me luck.

A couple of days after this Burns Supper, I was contacted by the midwife's partner who was a journalist with the Daily Record, Scotland's then leading tabloid daily paper. To be absolutely fair to this reporter, he said he had heard about my story from his partner and wondered if I would speak to him about it if we could meet for coffee. So I arranged to meet him in Glasgow for a coffee, and he said the paper was interested in doing an article on us. He reassured me that it would be very positive. After all the battles of the previous decade, I was flattered by the attention and was still in the heady state of having made history as the first single woman to gain access to fertility treatment in Scotland. Why not? It seemed like a good idea to me, and would raise the awareness of the issue and inequality of fertility treatment in Scotland. Did I think I needed to talk to anyone else first, like the press office of the Scottish Labour Party? It never crossed my mind. The only people I checked with first were the nurses and doctors at the hospital, as having allowed me access to treatment in Edinburgh, I did not want to jeopardise further treatment. They were absolutely fine about it.

On 14th Feb 1999, the front cover of the Daily Record had a lovely full page picture of us both hugging under the bold headline – *Labour's Test Tube Mum*. The editorial was, by agreement, very positive and it was a great picture. I had never expected our story to be front page news with several pages of follow up on the inside of the paper, but still a story worth telling, I thought. I was pleased, if somewhat taken aback by the full-on press coverage. After dropping you off at school and handing a copy of the newspaper in to the staffroom and speaking to your teacher, I had a meeting in Glasgow that day. As I walked through the railway station, there we were on the newspaper stands with our pictures splashed across the front page.

Then my mobile phone started to ring non-stop. The Labour Party went completely bonkers. Apparently, their press officer had some interesting industrial story about the closure of the local steel works lined up as the top story of the day. In Malcolm Tucker style, they were very pissed off indeed that I had knocked them off the front page.

The Daily Record Front Page from 15th February 1999
(reproduced with permission)

MAKE MINE A DOUBLE

If Carol can, then Canavan can too

By JOAN BURNIE

Lone mum uses same donor for a second IVF baby

EXCLUSIVE
By CARLOS ALBA and STEVE MARTIN

SINGLE mother Carol Fox plans to give the daughter she had through fertility treatment a biological double for a brother or sister.

She wants to give birth to a second IVF child using sperm from the donor who helped her have seven-year-old Natasha.

The Record revealed yesterday that Carol, 38, a Labour candidate for the Scottish parliament, was crying for a second baby.

The trade union official is delighted at the way life has turned out for her and Natasha.

Carol wants the closest blood possible between her children. So she will use sperm from the same donor to give her second baby the finest sperm for her original IVF treatment in England, and will have which half of it flown north.

Last night, she launched a passionate defence of her plans — while admitting that starting a family without a man in her life had left her out of pocket.

Carol, who contests Edinburgh West in May's Holyrood elections, said: "I think it is important for Natasha to have a full brother or sister. I will try to do that as long as the possibility exists.

"I have an eventful private life — but I have millions in credit at the sperm bank. The technicalities are not as important as the principle. I believe in a woman's right to choose to have children in whatever circumstances."

Carol hopes to be the first single mother to give birth to an IVF baby in Scotland.

Clinics here have traditionally refused to treat the single women or gay couples now accepted at many English fertility centres. Carol had to go to a Sussex clinic to have Natasha.

She believes having IVF treatment in a single mother has posed no threat to her Holyrood plans. She spoke about Natasha at her Labour selection interview.

Even if Carol does not win Edinburgh West — the Westminster version of the seat is held by the Liberal Democrats — the may still make a major impact in Labour circles. She has asked for the chance to speak about being a single mother at the party's Scottish conference next month.

If chosen, she may well touch on the once-taboo topic of infertility, a problem she has been struggling with since she was 20.

After several operations, she was told it was unlikely she could conceive. With time running out and with no sign of a suitable long-term partner, she opted for IVF.

Last night fertility campaigners offered her their support — and pointed out that the treatment, which has cost more than £15,000 so far, was being paid for by Carol herself, not the NHS.

MAYBE Dennis Canavan, the rejected Holyrood candidate, should have tried it...

Ditched his image as a family man, and told Labour's selection police that his proudest achievement was not everything he has done for his Falkirk constituents in his years as an MP, but the fact that he had chosen to be a test-tube dad.

Nothing would have proved his new Labour credentials more than being a man willing to spend £15,000 to be a father — without bothering with any of that old-fashioned, boy meets girl, falls in love stuff.

After all, it worked for Carol Fox, so why not for Dennis? IVF nance for the gender should surely be the same for the goose.

Not that there is anything particularly wrong in Carol Fox's decision. Nor will it count against her in her constituency.

She has the full-hearted support, at least officially, of her office-bearers, and a quick straw poll in Edinburgh west streets showed local people backed her too.

Only one middle-aged lady in Corstorphine thought it was: "Pretty much what I would expect of the Labour Party but then I will live and die a Tory."

In the meantime, Dennis, have you ever thought about donating some sperm?

Perhaps if you did, New Labour might just relent and let you get on that candidates' list.

LABOUR'S TEST TUBE MUM

HAPPY FAMILY: Carol is thrilled with her seven-year-old daughter Natasha, who wants to give her a biological brother or sister.
Picture: IAN TORRANCE

Should single mothers get this treatment?

YES
Sam Elliston
Ethics Lecturer

CLINICS have to take into account the welfare of any child that may be born as a result of the treatment.

They have to consider the need of the child for a father, is giving treatment to a single woman to a sin-gle woman is going to be a matter of discretion.

It would be a tremendous insult to single parents if it was thought that merely being single meant you were unable to parent adequately. It depends on the individual circumstances.

What matters is the welfare of the child. If the child is going to enter into a loving, supportive relationship with a single parent, we should not automatically see it is inappropriate. It should be weighed up on the merits of each case. No one has yet proved that having only one parent is harmful to a child.

There are many children with both a mother and father who have suffered dreadful neglect and abuse. Stereotyping doesn't really work — you have to look at the individual merits.

It depends on what we mean by parenting — whether we have a traditional mother and father role or accept that there are many different ways to bring up children these days.

NO
Cornelia Oddie, Family and Youth Concern

CHILDREN are not commodities to be obtained as part of a lifestyle package.

No one has the right to motherhood, least of all someone ready to embark on motherhood without providing optimum conditions for raising a child.

These conditions are a loving home with a mother and a father, who provide the care which each can offer at different times according to the changing needs of the child.

Babies need their mothers more, but as children grow older the father's role becomes increasingly important.

This is especially so with adolescent boys.

Girls from broken families are more at likely to become teenage mothers. Britain has the highest divorce rate in Europe. It also has the highest teenage pregnancy rate.

High rates of divorce and illegitimacy have created over one million single parent families, mostly headed by mothers.

Children from these families suffer not only from material deprivation, but from emotional and psychological problems which come from a lack of firm family structure.

Inside pages from The Daily Record of 16th February 1999
(reproduced with permission)

There I was, a hopeless candidate in an unwinnable seat, apparently smiling about being a deliberate single parent. You can imagine their delight. Worse still, the first party apparatchik who called me proceeded to lecture me about the adverse publicity for the party of me being a wilful single parent and that everyone was just furious with me. Apparently Helen Liddle, known locally in Scotland as Stalin's Grannie, was incandescent with rage. I was told that I should not speak to any other journalists and stop going on about being a single parent.

Now I could just about understand their ire that some "no mark" candidate in an unwinnable seat had disrupted the press strategy for the day, but this press officer most definitely crossed the line wanting to silence me about being a single parent. Firstly, I reminded her that I had a Scottish Labour Party policy document that said in black and white that, *"Scottish Labour respects all Scottish families in all their diversity."* I asked her if somehow this policy had been rescinded or was in fact entirely made up? I also reminded her that I had been completely open at the panel interview, even though I had never expected to be on the front page of the Daily Record. After that very difficult phone call, I was summoned to see the then General Secretary at party HQ in Glasgow.

I arrived to this dressing down to find that day's copy of the Daily Record absolutely covered with yellow post-it notes. It seemed there were very many stories in the Record at odds with Labour Party strategy that day, not just mine. After a tense discussion, I refused to give an undertaking that I would not speak to any more journalists but agreed that if I did I would at least give them some notice. As a candidate, I had been issued with a Labour Party pager and very bizarrely I then recall news alerts about myself and the party line to be adopted, along 'the lines – 'candidate causes controversy'. Response to be 'no comment - private matter - keep to the five pledges – story of the day - Scotland better under Labour.' *'God help us,'* I thought.

As I was leaving party HQ in Glasgow, some wee media laddie in a suit, who looked about twelve, on a short term contract to cover the press and radio at the crack of dawn every morning, stopped me. He wanted to give me the benefit of his thoughts and his take on my "story". He stood in front of me talking. Words were coming out of his mouth, but I didn't really hear a thing he said to me as I summoned up enough resolve to stay calm. I did absolutely everything in my power to stop myself thumping him there and then with the nearest placard. Now that would have been a story - *Candidate deselected and done for GBH as she brains Labour Party idiot* - if only!

How dare some sneering young man with no experience of life or adversity have the audacity to judge me, it was just about enough to push me over the edge. I was totally enraged, but breathed deeply and left. Driving home, I was the subject of radio bulletins and fodder for the day for the news commentators of Scotland. Shock horror, woman wants baby, hold the next front page.

My only real concern amidst all the furore was for you. I finished early so that I could pick you up from school. We had talked about the story in the newspaper and I had given a copy to your teacher when I dropped you off in the morning. The school had always been great and your teachers, especially Mrs. Laurie from P1 to P3, were very fond of you. I had been very open with you from a very young age and had written a story book when you were two and had updated this as the years had passed. All professional advice about assisted conception, which I had followed, was to be open and honest and explain in understandable language as your child started to ask questions. So you were, at six years old, a very confident outgoing child and you had already advised your friends in P1 that the doctor helped to make you. It was not news to anyone in our circle and I would not have contemplated doing anything which adversely affected your wellbeing.

Standing in the playground waiting for home time, a bit

shell shocked from the day, a few parents, mainly other mums came up to speak to me. They were all very positive and said they were sorry that I had had such troubles having children. They were all very encouraging. While I was waiting one mother came up to me and said, '*Saw that story in the paper and that, nice picture, good for you, but I didn't know that you were thirty-eight like ...* ' Most of the story had passed her by, but my age was utterly shocking. I laughed and walked home with you, secure in the knowledge that the ordinary Scottish public is far more sensible and sympathetic to the ups and downs of human life than the dubious people who spend their lives working for political parties, apparently trying to control the world.

The story did not end there. The paper was happy to have caused such controversy and kept it going for a few more days. I was summoned to yet another meeting of the local party in Edinburgh West to consider whether I should be deselected as their candidate. This was a very unpleasant interrogation by a very unpleasant chairman, who took it upon himself to give me a lecture on family values. This was no mean feat by him and completely outrageous as it was common knowledge at the time that he was engaged in extra- marital affairs with other members of the party. He was, however, overcome with rage and indignation that he had received a phone call from The Sun newspaper to ask whether I was gay. He did stop short of asking me that question directly as he would have had his head to play with in reply. How was that relevant, one way or the other? Had anyone actually read the article, about the operations, the exploding ovaries? I despaired and I certainly was not going to pander to his narrow minded prejudice and his misguided homophobic comments. He was for me the epitome of the right wing narrow minded hypocrisy of the party and he made me want to stand down there and then, so that I could tell the Labour Party where to shove their unwinnable seat.

However, my good friend and my agent Robert Bell, brought some sense and good humour back to this tense meeting, when he said he was pleased that the unwinnable seat of Edinburgh West had finally got a story on the front page of the Daily Record and it hadn't cost a penny! Robert was a great character and a wonderful agent. He planned to have a street party when he learned of Margaret Thatcher's demise and kept a drawer full of fireworks and rockets to set off for the occasion. Sadly, Robert predeceased Mrs. Thatcher.

The backlash to this press coverage did not, however end there, and it really is an education to receive hate mail quoting the bible IN CAPITAL LETTERS or to be accosted in the street with venom and prejudice. One such man came rushing up to me in St John's Road in Corstorphine and roared at me, right in my face, that he did not agree that lesbians should be allowed to adopt children! Someone else who had evidently not read the article about the wayward ovaries, but whose vote the Labour Party could perhaps afford to forgo. A few ignorant members of the public I can almost forgive, but the spineless hypocrites who disingenuously inhabit our political parties and pontificate from high on other peoples' lives, well frankly they make me sick.

So having made something of a public spectacle of my one and only remaining ovary, I returned with my head held high and my emotions in turmoil to attempt the twenty-second cycle of fertility treatment in March 1999. Again it involved the IVF drug regime, injections and scans and resulted in three more healthy looking embryos being implanted. At least, the two week wait was easier to bear with all the buzz of the first Scottish Parliament election.

I remained the candidate, and our small team of volunteers made the campaign as uplifting as possible in the sure knowledge that we couldn't win. Robert was great and very supportive, we travelled around in his car covered in posters with the loudspeaker imploring folk to vote Labour. At first, you were so embarrassed you hid face down in the back seat but once we were on quieter country roads, you were persuaded to take your chance with the loudspeaker. So you were seven when you first got involved in politics and implored people to vote Labour!

The constituency was a straight fight between the Tories and the Liberals. Lord James Douglas Hamilton was the candidate for the Tories and was in every way the epitome of an old school gent. '*Very good speech Carol, I must say, did you write that yourself, very good indeed.*' On the other hand, the female Liberal Democrat candidate seemed to wear the same jacket to every meeting, but changed her message each time to suit the audience. Robert told me he overheard her saying in aggrieved tones in 1999 that Edinburgh West could not have a gay MSP which I find just hilarious, as she herself was later very unpleasantly outed by the News of the World and now much later and unelected, lives happily in a Civil Partnership very involved in what is known as Civic Scotland. Politicians, don't you just love them?

The first Scottish Parliament elections took place in May 1999, and while the experience of being a candidate was not all pleasant it was, overall, a good experience and I learned a great deal. I was of course not elected, but was a healthy and respectable third. The Labour Party vote did not collapse at the advent of their single parent candidate.

Once, twice, three times **Labour**

But yet again, shortly afterwards, I was not pregnant. I said goodbye to another three embryos and set my sights very firmly on the future. After all, it was still early days in Scottish terms as I had only just started treatment in Edinburgh and as long as there is life in my one increasingly aged ovary, I resolved to keep going and aim for the next cycle.

Chapter 16

Treatment cycle number twenty-three in September 1999 came and went, as the three before. Again three good embryos but sadly, no pregnancy and no baby. I was exhausted, dejected and broke. I decided to take a break before I contemplated the plan for the year 2000 and becoming thirty-nine. Other accounts I have read of fertility treatment emphasise the injections, the invasive medical treatment, the roller coaster of emotions and the upset. I remember feeling crushingly disappointed, but would not allow myself to wallow in it, as I needed to summon up all my strength for the next time round. Fertility treatment is like a combination of running a marathon and the hurdles at the same time. You have to keep going but try only to focus on getting over the immediate hurdle ahead, because you don't know where the finishing line is, around the next corner or miles along the road? Besides which, I had a full-time job and you to look after, so I didn't have the luxury of giving in to my emotions or hiding under the duvet. I needed to be tough and keep going.

On Sunday 17th October 1999, I was filling up the car at the local garage in Edinburgh on our way to Motherwell to visit your grandparents. When I went inside to pay, the garage was doing a promotion, giving away free copies of The Sunday Times. Not a huge fan of this Rupert Murdoch newspaper, since the days of the Wapping trade union disputes, I nevertheless accepted a free copy. Later that night, having returned home and after you were in bed, I settled down to read the Sunday papers. On page 6 of the News Review there was a full broad sheet article by one Melanie Phillips with the bold headline: "*Women behaving disgracefully.*" The by-line underneath read, "*Women, not men, are driving a collapse in moral values that is undermining the family and ultimately themselves,*" says Melanie Phillips. This article was accompanied by a huge picture of a crowd of baying women at a male strip club. Another tedious article by a right wing woman in need of some serious conscious raising, I thought, and I was about to throw the newspaper in the bin, too tired to care about her anti-feminist rant, when I noticed a picture of Madonna and some comment about her status as a single parent. There to my utter surprise, about two thirds into the article was a paragraph where both my good self, *Carol Fox, Labour Party candidate and Madonna, rock icon,* were both roundly denounced for destroying the moral fabric of society due to our wanton single parenthood. I have never met Madonna, Rock icon, nor this journalist, apparently promoting her new book, but there I was being traduced in the very same breath as Madonna. You could not make it up.

Sadly some women, not part of any sisterhood, who make their living by sitting in judgment of others do not help to build anything much at all, as they write these articles and visit the studios of *Question Time* ranting about how other people should live their lives.

Needless to say, the publicity surrounding my reproductive battles coupled with my foray into politics did not go down well at work circles. I handed them, on a plate, some interesting ammunition which they stirred in the pot alongside my outrageous ambition to be an MSP. Clearly, in their eyes, this evidence proved that I was not dedicated enough, nor interested enough in the plight of their union or Scottish teachers.

For legal reasons alas, I cannot tell you much or go into details nor sadly name names. It is, however, a matter of public record that, following a formal complaint from me when I was unwilling to remain silent any longer (and had wisely amassed enough evidence), one individual was suspended from the union and following further discussions, I made the even wiser decision to leave. During the course of this extremely difficult period, a previously supportive official from England commented that I had lost my sparkle. My retort was that it was difficult to sparkle when you are wading through a sea

143

of shit every day. However, I decided it was in the end my individual responsibility to go off and find my sparkle again.

So, in the year 2000, at the start of the new millennium, I resolved to find a new professional direction *and* to keep trying to get pregnant. After all, I reassured myself I was by then only thirty-nine, which is the age most women *start* to have fertility treatment, even though I have been zapping my ovary with super hormones for a decade. In my low moments, I wanted to give up, for it all to be over, and certainly my friends and family regarded me as addicted to fertility treatment or possessed by a demon, or both. I could recognise from everyone else's standpoint that it did not seem logical, but on another level it was scientific, and there is always hope. There are better and better drugs and look, I argued to my doubters and myself, when all is said and done it worked before. It is only a matter of staying healthy and determined. It is only a matter of time. I WILL overcome. That is what I kept telling myself, and my circle of increasingly worried friends and family who didn't say anything, because the expression on their face said it all.

The millennium passed with three more IVF attempts. Number twenty-four, Jan 2000, number twenty-five in May 2000 and number twenty-six in September 2000, with three embryos each time transferred. None of these nine embryos stayed alive inside me, and another pregnancy became more and more elusive.

More than ever, I looked at you every day as the profound miracle that you are and it was hard for me to believe that I did get pregnant once. Whenever I was tempted to indulge in a twinge or even a moment of self pity, I berated myself to count my blessings and work hard to give you the best life I could. After all, I had to prove Melanie Phillips and her ilk wrong. I had to uphold the moral fabric of our society. Not to mention being a single parent while working full time. The right wing wrath of Melanie Phillips and others only made me more determined to keep going.

By now, you were your own spirited and lively self, equally determined to be in this world. Your embryonic brothers and sisters seemed to have had greater doubts and, either the science world or the spirit world, wasn't quite as it should be. I was wonderfully reassured by the fact that you were a happy and engaging child with a maturity far beyond your years. You also knew that I adored the very bones of you and your quick witted intelligence and strong will projected you forward each day without much apparent care about whether you had a brother or sister. At the time you felt much more deprived that we didn't have any pets, and held your ground over one particularly difficult weekend when you made your case and tried to wear me down to buy you a cat or dog. I did not relent but we settled on a hamster.

I was pleased that you were settled and happy. I remember you telling me about when you had sex education, you put your hand up to tell the teacher that was not the only way to make babies. You were quite proud when you came home from school one day after yet another sex education lesson. You told me that the teacher left the classroom for a few minutes and all the children were saying, '*Ewww, it sounds horrible and our mums and dads have done that, minging*'. Then Mohamed shouted in a loud voice, '*except Natasha's mum.*' You were so proud of my celebrity status in your class that day, I decided to hold off putting you right until you were older.

By this stage, it seemed very mysterious to me that I had ever managed to get pregnant and I tried to think myself back into positive thoughts and karma. I went for massages. I paid a therapist to make a tape where I spoke to Benjamin, the dark eyed, smiling baby boy I wanted to welcome into the world. I started to drink foul tasting tea again. I cut down (if not out) alcohol. I was possessed and it was becoming absurd.

You knew about my trips to the hospital. You remember coming to see me when I had the third ovarian cyst, worried why I was in hospital and that afterwards I couldn't pick you

145

up. You looked after me when I got home and left me little notes in big children's handwriting.

But for your sake, I tried to keep the failed cycles of disappointment to a very matter of fact, *'Oh well, never mind,'* I tried, but I didn't always succeed. Then bizarrely, your circle of friends at school, who were also only children, one after another announced that their mum was having a baby, all of these pregnancies with an eight year age gap. At school, your class were given a sheet to fill in headed *About me* and you wrote:

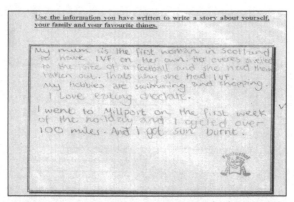

"My mum is the first woman in Scotland to have IVF on her own. Her overes swelled to the size of a football and she had them taken out. Thats why she had IVF.

My hobbies are swimming and shopping.

I love eating chocolate.

I went to Millport on the first week of the holidays and I cycled over 100 miles. I got sun burnt".

146

Coming to the end of the year 2000, after these six unsuccessful IVF attempts at Edinburgh, I was called in to see the consultant. He was kind and sympathetic. He knows, he said, that I am an intelligent and determined woman, he can see that, he respects that. But then, he looked me in the eye and solemnly said that he has to tell me that enough is enough. I was thirty-nine and there was now very little chance, after the last six IVF cycles, that I would get pregnant again and I needed to stop. But I protested. I told him that this has to be my decision and besides, there was sperm left. It would be such a waste not to use it. You never know, one more attempt just might work? Surely he couldn't deny me that, after all it was my body and I was paying? He looked stern faced, '*Yes I can,*' he said, '*and I must.*' He does.

I thought to myself (unfairly) that I must be adversely affecting their statistics of success, success being a take home baby, and that was why they were pulling the plug. I thought, '*They don't want me because my only ovary is now aged and while producing the eggs okay, the bun is never quite in the oven. But I have had doctors tell me all sorts over the years: I can't have kids at all, that I must not have a child out of wedlock, that I was too young to know my own mind and to have fertility treatment in London. Yet, I had a baby at thirty-one in London. It is only a matter of time. I will prove them all wrong again.*' I was upset, but defiant and determined which only served to reinforce his belief that he needed to make the decision for me. I was shown the door. I marched home angry and I howled in private when you were asleep in bed.

I felt so angry that I couldn't get pregnant again at thirty-nine that I decided to become a lawyer. Does that sound strange? I wanted to be in control of something that I could achieve. So, I left my job as a trade union official. Maybe it was all the hormones I was injecting at the time, but, I thought, I had hit upon a fairly brilliant idea. I would become a lawyer and fight for equality for others. For me anyway, it seemed easier to become a lawyer at thirty-nine than a mother again.

While the science can be absolutely brilliant and outrageously expensive, pregnancy can remain elusive.

Time to exercise my brain once more.

Chapter 17

In September 2000, I started a fast track postgraduate law degree. When I had first applied, I explained that I was a single parent and that I wanted to do the two year, fast track, law degree while working part-time. I was told flatly that this was just not possible, as it would just be much too difficult. Instead, I was advised to do the part-time degree run over six years.

Once more, I railed against people in authority telling me how to live my life, who, somehow, think they know better. I stressed that at thirty-nine, I had no intention of doing any six year degree. We finally agreed that they could take the fees for the first year of the two year degree and, if they were right, they could just keep the money and wait for me to fail. I started the degree in September 2000, following the last failed cycle of fertility treatment. You proudly announced to the world, *'My mum is going to be a lawyer now, like Ally McBeal, except for the thin part!'*

I couldn't afford not to work, so after sending my CV around and keeping my eye on the newspapers, I obtained a part-time job with the Equal Opportunities Commission in Glasgow. I worked half the week as a job-sharer, and the other half I concertinaed my law lectures and tutorials into very long days. Isobel gallantly came to the house at 7 am every Monday morning to let me leave early and she took you to school. Meanwhile, I took a flask and sandwiches to keep me going through back to back lectures and tutorials. I scared the living daylights out of the undergraduate students, who appeared to spend most of their time either in the refectory drinking coffee or endlessly highlighting passages in books, chatting and photocopying legal cases in the library.

Our friends and family helped out with the school run and babysat if I was working or studying late. But I soon created a double life and did a double shift, like your Nana before me. I was your mother first and made sure we had normal evenings

149

together doing your homework, settling down to watch TV and only when you were asleep did I start to study at 9 pm regularly until 2 or 3 am. I wanted to prove them all wrong. I wanted to prove *the world* wrong. I never missed an essay deadline or failed an exam. I survived on three or four hours sleep a night. I even won the bursary for the best marks of the graduate students, proving those who wanted to shunt me and my weary mature student brain to the side track of the six year degree well and truly wrong. Little did they know that if I couldn't have another baby, then I was most certainly going to have a law degree and pretty damn quick. That at least was within my control. I took all my energy and determination in hand and tried to think about the future, and not about the babies that hadn't happened.

Money was again extremely tight, but I had long since become accustomed to debt. A law degree was, I thought, very good debt indeed. It was not shoes. We will be okay, I told myself. Despite this positive mental attitude, I had a call from the Inland Revenue as they thought something was very wrong as my salary has reduced dramatically to £9,000 per year. It's okay, I told them, I was working part-time but I had a five year plan and I was going to be a lawyer. Part of this plan had to involve sharing your bunk bed and renting out my room to international students who studied English in Edinburgh. We amassed a nice collection of coffee table books from around the world and the house was a cosmopolitan hive of activity. Sometimes you complained and worried that we were poor, but I reassured you that it would all be worthwhile in the end and not to worry.

In January 2001, I turned forty. It was indeed a landmark but I had very mixed feelings as my only ovary must also now be forty, and its defunct companion had fortunately yet to make another miraculous and malfunctioning appearance. I arranged a long weekend in New York for my birthday and I tried to enjoy myself, despite a raging dose of the flu. I trailed up and down Manhattan and had a coffee at the very top of the twin towers in January 2001. When I came back, I tried a dose of "fuck you" bravado and decided to hold a "Feisty Feminist Fox is Forty" party. I imagined a gathering of intellectual feminists debating serious and important matters over sophisticated cocktails. Unfortunately, those with bad timing arrived very late and already a bit drunk so it wasn't quite how I imagined.

Meanwhile, Simone was talking about returning from Canada to England the following year, so I dusted down a credit card and we went to visit her and Elliott in Vancouver in July 2001. This last holiday to Canada was not a complete success. Simone and Elliott had been to see us in Edinburgh a few years before which had been fine, but this time you kids bickered constantly, always over Harry Potter books and tapes. I had warned you that if you wanted to take the new tapes, you had to share them. You were very good, but Elliott was older and he wanted to race ahead listening to them by himself not with you. By the end of that holiday, I hated that bloody boy wizard and J.K. Rowling. It is interesting that so many years later Emma Watson has declared herself a passionate advocate for equality at the United Nations. Alas, there is still no spell to ward off the evils of the patriarchy.

While we were on holiday in Canada Simone had to work, so I was left looking after arguing kids, for long stretches in unfamiliar surroundings. Life had been hard for Simone in many ways, but on the last night of that holiday we had a terrible row about being single parents. Angry about her own disappointments in life, she said that it had all been *so* much *easier* for me because I had chosen to be a single parent while it has been unremittingly hard for her.

I was utterly dismayed that our previous unconventional London family was in the past and she now saw our lives as in some sort of competition. I replied that life can be hard for us all, but we just needed to make the best of whatever hand life deals us. The atmosphere was tense and awful as we

151

said goodbye at the airport the next morning. We were both angry with life but we parted angry with each other and the geographical distance reinforced an emotional distance that neither of us ever, properly, attempted to bridge. Although our friendship suffered, I ensured that I remained in touch with Elliott. After all, I loved my godson and had looked after him when he was little. I kept sending his birthday and Christmas money with the odd football t-shirt and books with rude Scottish words which he loved. We stayed in touch but after that it was never quite the same again, an important friendship tested and damaged by an unnecessary argument about the difficulties of being single parents. *'Why, oh why, do mothers fight about who does it best?'* I wondered.

Being a mother is wonderful, but it can also be very difficult and, sadly, hellish for some, but we need to support each other rather than engage in pointless 'Mummy wars'. But it is easy to fall into that man-made trap just because we want to do the very best for our children and being a single parent puts double the pressure on one pair of shoulders. I was more able to shrug off those pressures, while Simone struggled with the expectations of others, even though Elliott was musically gifted and fluent in French, reading those thick Harry Potter books in French from a young age.

Natasha, Simone and Elliot in Canada

When we returned home from Canada in 2001, nearly a year after the last failed cycle, I resolved to contact Dr. Robertson in Eastbourne to see if I could go back there for further treatment. If he says no, I tell myself, I will accept it. I trust him more than any other doctor of my acquaintance, then or since. He fully understands my need to keep trying, while there is still hope. He says he will help me to try again, and we arrange to transfer the sperm back to Eastbourne. Ping pong sperm, on its return journey from Scotland to the South of England. This doctor and the furthest South of England were once more hospitable to me.

I finished the first year of the law degree, tried to gather together my emotional and financial resources (as ever with the help of my by now completely baffled parents), and I headed to Eastbourne for attempt number twenty-seven in August 2001. Fertility treatment was by then, part of my personae, part of who I was, and what I was about in the world and I was prepared to travel to the ends of the earth.

Cycle number twenty-seven of IVF in Eastbourne was a fairly straight forward and routine affair: injections, scans, anaesthetics, operations. By then, I was blasé. So blasé, that I got back to Gatwick and flew back up, by myself, after the anaesthetic. I avoided looking at my three embryos down the telescope as it always made it all the harder to realise that something is alive, a small ball of happy cells, beating and dividing away, waiting for a comfortable home in my uterus. I recall again the last year of primary school and the endless reproductive talks and questions. '*Please miss what exactly is a uterus for when it doesn't bloody work?*' I wanted to ask then. '*Breathe, breathe, think positive thoughts.*' Wait two weeks.

Pregnant?

Nope.

Cycle number twenty-eight of IVF in September 2001 – same again and three more embryos. By now, it feels like I

153

am heading for an entry in the Guinness Book of Records. My ovary has been zapped into oblivion, but still manages to produce eggs. The sperm is of course excellent. I am told this again and again. I am the problem. But this occasion did not make a baby despite the fancy surroundings, the white coats and the scary money. It is frankly desperate. And I was still busy being a single parent, working part-time with the Equal Opportunities Commission, doing a fast track law degree and commuting from Scotland to the South of England for fertility treatment. My life was full on madness. I can recognise this now, but I didn't then. I just wanted everything to fall into place. No joy with cycle twenty-eight either, and three more embryos gone.

Then a further medical condition intervened once more, when I developed an incisional hernia. This basically meant that I had been cut open so often that my insides started to fall out and bulge out from places they shouldn't. Charming. I was once again admitted to the Edinburgh Royal Infirmary for a further abdominal operation in September 2001.

While I was recovering from this last operation, I had a phone call to contact Eastbourne as a matter of urgency.

It transpired that the sperm frozen in 1991 was now dangerously close to its sell by date, as the HFEA regulations only allow it to be stored for ten years. I had to arrange the next treatment cycle very quickly before the clinic (and all the doctors and staff I have come to respect) were done for serious criminal activity for helping an aged ovary make a baby, with out of date sperm. No wonder I had to write this book.

With my stitches from the hernia operation not yet removed I headed south for IVF treatment number twenty-nine. The same regime of injections, scans and egg retrieval with three more embryos replaced, although the official guidelines recommend no more than two, now due to the chance of multiple pregnancy. In my case, some chance. This was now the very last try, at least in the UK and I pray to God, Jesus,

Mary *and* Joseph, or frankly whoever will listen to let this be, the final glorious end, an end with a bang and not a whimper. I prayed for a blue dot or pink line.

Alas, there was no pink or blue, and it was the deflated end to a very long journey which started twelve years before.

It felt like a very untidy and a very sad ending. I don't do dark moments or sad endings. One vial of sperm remained, but as it was now passed its sell by date it could not be legally used in the UK. I asked Dr. Robertson to seek a stay of execution from the HFEA so that it would not be destroyed. It truly bothered me that I had had twenty-nine cycles of treatment. It did not seem right to end this journey on such an uneven number. I thought it might be altogether more symmetrical, more neat and tidy to end on thirty, a round number after all. I was forty and I could end on thirty cycles of treatment.

Round numbers have a certain invincible feminist ring to them, I thought.

My only choice by that stage was to go to court and challenge the HFEA to release the sperm and take my last vial to Belgium or America. I took some fairly feeble legal advice about mounting a human rights challenge and thought it over for a few days. I had managed to get myself to the South of England, but somehow I could not see me and my desperate hopes for further motherhood boarding a plane to go to Belgium or America. That did seem altogether desperate.

It was indeed the end.

This invincible feminist cried buckets for days. At home and even at work, I remember being heartbroken in the office of the Equal Opportunities Commission with concerned colleagues coughing loudly through the flimsy walls. Equal Opportunities, indeed! Any chance of future motherhood, gone. It really was the end of the fertility road. I was so very sad, broke and broken hearted as I had been convinced that my sheer determination and willpower would see me through to abundant motherhood. Alas, sheer willpower was not enough.

In summary, then dearest daughter, if you have stayed with me through all these reproductive ups and downs, I started having fertility treatment in May 1990 and I finally stopped in 2001. I had twenty-nine cycles of treatment, twelve cycles of fertility treatment before I became your mother, I had you, my wonderful, miraculous, beautiful daughter, then I tried, with all my heart and resolve, to have another baby, to give you a brother or sister, another seventeen times through GIFT, IVF, embryo transfers and anything that medical science had to offer at the time. I made forty-nine embryos which, for whatever reason, did not become babies.

I was sad about this for a very long time. I could no longer read any articles about IVF, and it was so hard to close that chapter of my life, on my fertility and hopes of more children.

I had no choice but to pack up these troubles quickly. I resolved again to focus upon you, and upon giving you the very best future I could. I did not want you to grow up feeling sad about what we did not have. I wanted you to grab life by the throat and live life to the full, determined to wring out every single drop of opportunity for what you wanted for your life, knowing I would be there to support you every step of the way.

I like action plans and lists. I have never been someone who wallows in self-pity and neither do I seek such pity or sympathy. I have written this story for you because I felt compelled to write it all down perhaps, not only for you but for any grandchildren to come, perhaps also for others who want children. After a short period of feeling low, I picked myself up and decided I would indeed become the best campaigning equality lawyer and single mother Scotland had ever seen. Or at least I would try.

I have a very large file of papers for you, which are kept in my wooden blanket box in my bedroom under my small flat screen TV, my books and box sets. Like a dedicated campaigner, I have kept all my medical records, every receipt for the medical treatment and travel costs but have never dared to add it up. I don't want to know. In trying to write this story for you, I have also bought and read lots of memoirs. The Scottish author, Candia McWilliams, has written about her unusual eye problems resulting in blindness and her fights with doctors for proper medical treatment for her rare condition. She eventually had to go private and she writes about how much her private treatment cost. Her pedigree cat cost her £350. So she writes about how much her private medical treatment cost her in numbers of pedigree cats. I can't begin to guess how many pedigree cats or dogs worth of fertility treatment I had over more than a decade. I do know that your Papa's garage would not be falling down if he had that pot of money to hand, but not once have any of us regretted the costs because it had to be done. It was a journey which had to be completed and you, beyond all expectations, are the prize that we all treasure.

Headline from Scotland on Sunday, 31st October 1999

Last hope in bid to complete IVF family

Time running out for single mother who caused a storm during the Holyrood election

Chapter 18

As my fertility journey ended, another journey began, into the conservative and arcane world of the Scottish legal establishment. All was going well, and I was due to graduate with my fast track law degree in June 2002. As a result of my experience as a full-time trade union official dealing with employment law in London and Scotland, my Labour Party links and the law degree, I was head hunted by a firm of trade union solicitors in January 2002. I left the Equal Opportunities Commission. One of the senior partners at the firm, who had vision and integrity, became my mentor and I was delighted to be offered the opportunity to work with this law firm, as it seemed then like an ideal fit.

With promised partnership on the distant horizons, I agreed to work part-time while completing the last part of my law degree. The next five year plan appeared to be working out. Given that I had already spent a decade dealing with employment law as a trade union official, I wanted to build upon this specialism as a solicitor. In particular, I wanted to focus upon equality law as my own experience had highlighted for me the dearth of claimant focused equality lawyers north of the border. What can be taken entirely for granted in London was, and still is, a struggle in Scotland. So I devoted all my attention to you and to this new and challenging chapter in my life, very much facing forward, not allowing myself to look back. I had been lucky enough to have one child and I was focused on achieving success for you and for me. Every day I looked at you and realised just how lucky I was. Anything else in life would be a bonus.

The day of my last exam in the law degree arrived. I was the epitome of my well organised self, glad finally, to have reached the end of two very demanding years. Up early, as usual, I had everything organised to drop you off at school and to get to Glasgow for the exam. Teeth brushed and coats on, we were ready, just about to leave the house shortly after 8 am when you decided to go to the toilet and accidently shut your finger in the bathroom door. You let out the loudest scream imaginable and I rushed upstairs wondering what the hell had happened. You were crying and sobbing loudly and you held up a very sore finger. Conscious of the time, and my last exam, I tried my best to calm you down running your sore finger under the cold tap, all the while reassuring you that you could go to school, trying to edge towards the door. I was blowing on your finger telling you everything was going to be fine when you looked at me and went chalk white. Then, in a split second, you projectile vomited all over the bedroom.

We both just stood there in shock for a few seconds surrounded by vomit, cuddling each other, you crying and me thinking that my career in law was about to be sabotaged at the last hurdle by an unexpected sea of sickness. I imagined all those smug faces of officialdom who had said it couldn't be done, that I was too ambitious for my own good, uppity single parent that I was. Bastards, I thought, what the hell do they know?

After five minutes when you had finally calmed down, I almost admitted defeat. I saw the clock ticking away and realised that you would not be able to go to school. I felt my brilliant future legal career slip from my grasp. Then in a flash of activity I folded up the bedspread full of vomit, threw it into a black bag, quickly changed your clothes and bundled us and everything into the car (including the black bag full of sick). I frantically called Nana, telling her that we were on our way to her house. Nana, being a wonderful nurse, was always a godsend in these circumstances. I drove from Edinburgh like a bat out of hell to Motherwell, deposited a very pale child with a throbbing sore finger and a bag of sick on her door step and headed for the motorway to Glasgow. I made it to the exam hall with minutes to spare and had to calm myself down sufficiently to answer questions on such earth shatteringly important topics as the Law of the Tenement in

Scotland, all the time hoping that Nurse Nana had dealt with your medical emergency. When I collected you later, your finger was bandaged up and you told me you had an operation. The doctor had to pierce your nail with a needle and then tape up your finger. You also met lots of Nana's friends at the health centre who gave you pound coins for being brave. You remember that day as me being too busy to look after you and not caring about your sore finger. I remember a stressful day, trying to keep all the balls in the air and our future on track.

I passed the exams and graduated at age forty-one with my law degree. I had a clear focus and plan of where I wanted to go as I elbowed my way into my new profession and career number three. Little did I realise that if you fail to follow the conventional path into law, from private school to university and then in your early twenties straight to a traineeship, many further obstacles are placed in your way and sour opprobrium is heaped upon you from a great height by unimaginative people who believe the world turns on its axis, only if we all follow the same conventional path and don't ask awkward questions.

The next step after the Law Degree to become a Scottish solicitor was to undertake a further year at university doing the Diploma in Legal Practice at a cost of a further £4,000. I had no more money than anyone else over the years, but I have had a more relaxed attitude to debt and to short term risk, always believing that my ability to work hard would see us alright. As well as the further financial hurdle, the diploma presented there was also a requirement to become a full-time student. I knew immediately that this would not be possible for me as a single parent, because I needed to work at least part-time. I contacted both the Law Society of Scotland and the university for advice.

Both institutions were singularly unhelpful and frankly very uninterested in the plight of some "Jeannie-come-lately", mature student, single parent who had the fanciful idea of becoming a lawyer over forty. You could hear the sneer of contempt in their voices as I explained my predicament. I clearly did not know my place and had to be put back into it as sharply as possible. I remember being told on the phone, by a very haughty official, that I would have to become a full-time student and do the diploma just like everyone else before she hung up abruptly.

Fortunately for me, and for you, the instinct from my much younger days, of fighting back and chasing someone down the street to knock their block off, has remained embedded in my psyche. Thus far, as an adult I have not yet acted on that final impulse (despite almost daily provocation), but I do still get extremely pissed off and angry with individuals who lack the courage and imagination to fully live their own lives, yet somehow judge or determine the rules by which the rest of us should live ours. Not on your Nellie.

Older and wiser, I perhaps choose my battles better these days, but I nearly always fight back somehow, and in every case, either mine or my clients, I never *ever* settle for two balloons and a whistle. Neither should you, not ever. It is important in life to have the courage of your convictions.

Despite this hostile and unhelpful response from the Law Society of Scotland, I then requested a copy of the Solicitors' Admission Regulations and undertook further research myself. After several hours of reading I found an alternative path. There in black and white was a reference to a non-diploma training contract which neither the university, nor the Law Society had even bothered to tell me about. It seemed to me that vested interests and closed shops were not only the province of trade unions. So, with the support of my senior partner in Edinburgh, I immediately wrote to the Law Society of Scotland, seeking access to this route to qualifying as a solicitor.

Aghast at my further audacity, I was told that I could not apply, that this was the decision of the Law Society and I had to set out a case as to why I was exceptional and could not follow the conventional path. I replied, asking what criteria they used for assessing exceptional applications, but was told they had no such criteria, that I had to make my own case. I asked about their equal opportunities policy and was advised by the training department that this was beyond their remit. I encountered dead ends and brick walls all around. However, having come this far, I was not yet ready to give up.

I formally applied to be allowed this alternative route to becoming a solicitor, but the answer was no. I served a Sex Discrimination Questionnaire and found out that since 1982, only about six people in Scotland had previously been allowed this alternative route to qualifying. The very real barriers of childcare and lack of money did not even register with the privileged legal classes, and my application was turned down.

Disappointed and enraged, I started the diploma as required in October 2002, in the hope that I could (as with the law degree) work part-time, be a part-time student and do most of the studying in my own time late into evenings and at weekends around childcare and other domestic demands. The situation was just absurd. I had to leave the work I was doing in a real law firm to go to the university to take part in role play exercises in a virtual law firm. Lots of new technology for sure, and new theories of learning, but it seemed to make absolutely no bloody common sense.

Then six weeks into the diploma, my name appeared on the university notice board and I was asked to see the head of department. He advised me that while he was sympathetic to my situation, as a single parent and the fact that I needed to work, my attendance at the university was not satisfactory, as I had to be there 75% of the time or I would fail. I could pay the further £4,000, even again obtain the best marks, and yet still fail the course because I was a mother with childcare responsibilities. I was furious, like one of those cartoon characters with steam coming out of my ears. I told him that I would take legal advice.

In the circumstances, I had very little choice. I withdrew from the diploma, requested my money back and had to repay a grant I had been awarded from a charitable foundation. It looked like my journey towards becoming a lawyer had hit a dead end. But after a few days of being angry, I calmed down and I took legal advice. I had no other option but to sue the Law Society of Scotland. I was weary that I had to revert to litigation and take on another establishment to overcome stupid bloody obstacles erected (in the main) by stupid bloody men.

Most of my colleagues in the law firm thought I had lost my marbles. They thought that I had seriously gone over the top one last time. The received wisdom of the day was never to upset the Law Society of Scotland as they regulated the profession and would hang trouble makers out to dry at the first sniff of a complaint from a dissatisfied client. In turn, I was astounded by the number of supposed left wing, so called radical and campaigning lawyers who appeared to be scared shitless of the Law Society. From their point of view, they advised against suing the regulating body of solicitors before I had even joined the profession. So many educated and intelligent people, and yet, so little backbone, I thought. A few people offered quiet words of support but kept their own heads well and truly down.

Despite this general attitude, I did manage to find one very helpful Scottish solicitor who was not cowed by his masters and he helped me take a case of sex discrimination against the Law Society of Scotland. None of this is confidential and I have written newspaper articles about this particular battle to try to widen access to, and equal opportunities within, the legal profession in Scotland. The legal case took over a year before the Law Society finally backed down and changed their minds granting me an exemption from undertaking the diploma on condition that I undertake further Law Society exams at £40 per exam. Ironically, one of the exams was on Law and Ethics, but I thought better of writing a treatise on how it could be considered unethical not to publish a less expensive route to qualifying as a solicitor. I passed three more exams in Ethics, Court Procedures and Accounts. I was ushered into a room on my own and watched over by a Law Society official while I sat the exams. Not perhaps how to win friends and influence people, but I focused on passing the exams and getting to the next stage. Although I was still working in the law firm while I took the case, I lost a very valuable year of my over forty life. I have absolutely no respect for law makers and bureaucrats who make such ridiculous rules, but have never faced adversity or obstacles in their own smooth path to high office and power. Then they scratch their polished heads and wonder why they cannot connect with ordinary people?

While this particular battle and legal case was raging, a further Scottish Parliament election was due in May 2003. I was approached again by the Edinburgh West Constituency to ask if I would stand a second time as their candidate. While I was flattered, I was under no illusions that there would be any stiff competition for this particular unwinnable gig. I was still working full-time in the law firm but the partner in Glasgow was unenthusiastic about this further foray into Scottish politics, even though, due to the court case against the Law Society, my law career and five year plan were far from settled. So, somewhat bizarrely, I had to use my precious annual leave from a trade union law firm to stand as a Labour Party candidate. I also had to put my phone bill onto a budget account, as most of the campaigning was undertaken and funded privately by candidates themselves and I could only afford it with the help of my overdraft and flexible friends.

The 2003 campaign was tough going, with even fewer volunteers, covering a huge constituency. I caused less controversy this time around as I was, frankly, much too busy trying to get through each day. I was, however, told off once again by the Labour Party for agreeing to be photographed with Colin, who was standing as a list candidate for the Scottish Socialist Party. '*Have you ever had a brother who is a socialist? If the answer is "yes" then you must pass him on the street and do not under any circumstances have your picture taken with him for the newspapers.*' Absurd stuff, these party organisers are indeed a breed apart.

My success of 2003 was winning the legal case against the Law Society of Scotland. Colin's success of that same year was being elected to the Scottish Parliament as one of six Scottish Socialist MSPs. A TV news clip of him running around the counting hall, jumping up and kicking his heels was later replayed on *Have I Got News For You*. As the only one of his six erstwhile comrades who had not been arrested or been to jail, he was then elected to sit on the Justice Committee of the Scottish Parliament. He was a very conscientious MSP who was well respected and personable and gained support across the political spectrum. For my part, despite all my own previous battles, I then became known as 'Colin's sister', and many, due to his youthful appearance and dark hair, assumed he was my younger brother! Touché. Unfortunately, due to the scandalous megalomania and sexual antics of one Mr. Tommy Sheridan, all six of those MSPs lost their seats in 2007. But that is, most definitely, another story.

From 2003 until 2006, I concentrated on finally qualifying as a solicitor working full-time, using my previous experience, taking discrimination and equality cases to employment tribunals throughout Scotland. I had to carefully designate myself as a trainee solicitor, the oldest trainee in town perhaps? But I was always very careful to ensure that I kept on the right side of the Law Society. It often surprised those on the other side who turned up expecting a young "wet behind the ears trainee" only to find me sitting there, a grey haired old harpie.

During these years, you were growing up, heading for high school and emerging as a very early teenager with your own opinions and ideas. My total focus in life was to work hard to give you, my only child, the best possible start in life. I tried to ensure that you acquired the self confidence and optimism needed to deal with life's battles and to forge ahead towards your own path in life. Initially, you wanted to be a police woman and get a high up job like on *The Bill*. Then you transferred your attention to *ER* and wanted to be either a paediatrician, like George Clooney, or maybe a singer as you knew all the Disney songs by heart. You stuck in at school as you were clever and artistic and you also developed normal teenage interests in clothes, make up and going out. Above all, your intelligence and maturity shone through and you had a wide range of friends and an increasingly busy social life of activities with endless sleepovers.

Looking back, it was far from easy, working full-time, studying, being a single parent to a growing and independent minded teenager and generally making ends meet. But parenthood, being your mum, always gave me the utter focus and purpose that I needed to overcome the daily demands and exhaustion. I was also determined, having set out on a new path, to make a success of my new career. I was propelled forward by the previous decade of disappointments and was also reassured by the right noises coming from the partners

166

in the law firm that hard work and determination would be recognised and rewarded, and at that stage at least I had no reason to disbelieve them.

In 2004, you had started high school and met lots of new friends. You had been at nursery since you were six months old, then primary school and After School Club. Now at high school you soon had a wide circle of new friends. Amongst your new group of friends were twin girls, aged twelve, whose mum did not work, although now they were at high school she was considering getting a part-time job. This was a wholly new concept to you, that some mums stayed at home and did not have a paid job. For that first year of sleepovers with these new girls, I was bombarded by your new found criticisms of my approach to motherhood. Why did I not stay home and bake cakes? Why could I not be a normal mother? How did everyone else have a normal family? I got it in the neck for a sustained period of time which was neither pleasant nor easy, but I reassured myself that I was doing my best and that all would work out fine. Best, I thought, to focus on the bigger picture and the longer term, breathe through the daily upsets, then reach for a nice glass of wine or gin at the end of the day.

Besides, it reminded me of the hard time I had given my own mum when she worked nights to look after other sick children. As children, we only think of our own immediate needs but it is the adults around who have to keep the show on the road and I tried my best. You told me a few years ago that you felt bad and apologised for giving me such a hard time about, amongst other things, not making cakes. I reminded you that you were only a child and that, in my own time, I had also made my mum's life very difficult. It is all just part of the journey, even if the road becomes very difficult at times.

So began the bumpy journey and pressure of your teenage years, questioning and pushing against boundaries and the upheaval and intensity associated with teenage emotions. At the time, I had my head down working hard and looking to

167

the future. I couldn't even think about the past and my fertility journey. For me, the disappointment and sadness of not being able to have another child was too raw, it was still all too disappointing. That approach clashed and collided head on with your increasing curiosity and need to ask questions about the donor and fertility treatment from your perspective.

At high school you began to feel less special, and more different. Sometimes, you could not be consoled by the explanations that you were so loved, so wanted and so special and that you were here against all the odds. You grew angry with me, although I tried to remain calm, I didn't always handle things well, we fought and argued and you were often upset. It was so very difficult, coping with your distress and confusion. I tried my best to be reassuring and attentive, but found it very hard to know how to deal with our story from your perspective. My previous resolve that I was enough, that being open and honest with you, giving you everything in life faltered as you wanted the one thing I had not given you. You wanted to know more about your donor and we talked a lot about how we would tackle this for you.

To help me deal with these difficulties, I joined an organisation called the Donor Conception Network (DCN). In March 2006, we arranged to go to a meeting in London. Nana came with us and I left it open about how we would deal with the meeting and this next step. In the end, bonding over girly pursuits, daughter and granny decided that you would rather go shopping to Oxford Street, so I was sent off on my own to the meeting. Although this was then the single most important issue in your teenage life (and could be the subject of great distress), the pull of a shopping trip in London for a thirten year old was understandably even greater.

That Saturday morning, I set off on the London underground to find my way to a community centre in North London and got a bit lost. Standing outside the tube, consulting my map for directions, I bumped into some people with the same map and papers in their hands on their way to the same meeting. They had come down from Edinburgh that morning, especially for the meeting, and that was how I then met other single mothers by choice living in Edinburgh.

I was amazed, pleased but flabbergasted by their stories, and the relative ease with which they had become mothers. Of course, all the children were so much younger than you, babies and toddlers, and I was certainly the elder stateswoman of the group with a teenager. So we formed a support group in Edinburgh and met regularly. While I was roughly the same age as the other mothers with a few years difference, the age gap between the kids was more difficult, especially as they were all in the early balmy days of joy of being mothers, adoring their babies. I didn't think they wanted yet to know of the other side of the story, when the children were older and the road became rather more rocky. At first, you enjoyed these meetings, playing with the babies and answering the other mums' questions but you were at a very different stage and your needs were different. You were very upset at the last meeting in our house when a very new single mum came and told her story about having gone abroad for fertility treatment with donated eggs and sperm. She went into a lot of detail about her birth story and you left the room. I went after you to see what was wrong, as you weren't your chatty and outgoing self. You saw her story from the baby's perspective and you were angry and upset that nobody had asked the baby what he wanted. You thought it was going to be so much harder for that wee boy to find his donors, as they weren't in Scotland or even in England or Wales. You were just furious with that mum, and when I asked in the kitchen why you were so upset, you said, *'That wee baby has got it doubly worse than me and a mother who likes telling her story even more than you, she went on and on about her problems and being in hospital. What about the baby, what about his story? You mothers don't get it!'*

After that meeting, you cried really hard about that baby and I remember spending that night with you, trying to reassure you that this new baby would be well loved and looked after. But from your perspective at that time, you thought all the attention was on mothers and not enough on the children. After that, you didn't want to go to any more meetings and although I went along by myself to a few more coffee mornings and lunches, the gulf was too wide. Besides for me, by then, I was well past any campaigning mode. I was trying to deal with my own grief and disappointment by not facing it and putting it all behind me while you wanted to face it *all* head on, and forge ahead with your questions and your journey.

What was utterly amazing to me, was that all my new found friends had become pregnant fairly easily and more staggeringly for me had had their fertility treatment on the NHS. I couldn't believe it, even IVF on the NHS! Meanwhile they couldn't believe my horror stories about my fertility treatment and my being forced to leave Scotland to get access to fertility treatment as a single woman. It seemed that attitudes in Scotland had indeed changed. Changes wrought *not* by politicians, I hasten to add, but by women themselves, including me, making choices and being determined to become mothers.

In addition to joining DCN and then forming this support group to try to help you, I contacted the Human Embryology and Fertilisation Authority in London (HFEA). The legislation allowed for non-identifiable details of the donor to be released to the child when they turned eighteen, and also allowed voluntary contact with any siblings. So although you were too young, we registered your interest and I continued to give you what support I could, even though from your perspective it was often inadequate. Our tangled emotions on the subject meant that you felt angry and resentful towards me and more generally towards the world. You had another dimension of life to deal with, in addition to the normal trials and tribulations of teenage life. It was very hard for you and you often felt that you had no one else to turn to. Your strong character, your maturity then and your sense of yourself now, have been hard

170

won as you often felt alone and misunderstood then, no matter how hard I tried. I wanted your unhappiness to go away and not confront me. I wanted this to be our happy ending with no tears. For me, you are my happy ending. But it just wasn't the same happy ending for you.

Over the years, I have had to come to accept that, from your perspective, there is a sense of sadness and a longing that I do not share. I've tried my very best to understand. Looking back to my social work training and dealing with adoption cases, I appreciated that you would be curious about your other biological parent. When I was a social work student, I wrote my dissertation on adoption from the perspective of the birth mother. I read harrowing accounts in *The Adoption Papers* and since then have read lots of memoirs about adoption from Jackie Kay, A. M. Holmes and Jeanette Winterston. No matter how happy their childhood, adopted children always retain a curiosity about their biological beginnings. I appreciated that you would experience this curiosity too, in half measures at least. When you are ready, if you want, you can read the stories of Jackie Kay, whose biological parents both turned out to be fervently religious, while she was raised by Glaswegian communists. Or A.M. Holmes, adopted and raised in America by intellectual middle class parents who were told little more than, "*Your package has arrived, its wrapped in pink ribbons and has ten fingers and ten toes.*" Or the more harrowing tale of Jeanette Winterston who was adopted by an evil woman, a Jehovah's Witness, consumed by the thought that God had led her to the "wrong crib", which resulted in a loveless and abusive childhood for young Jeanette.

Yet, through our most difficult times, I consoled myself that our circumstances were different. There was no element of rejection for a start. You were so wanted and so loved. Even the donor had consented and gave his gametes to create life. He was anonymous because of the law but his actions helped to create you. So no one walked away or gave you away. The exact opposite in fact, as I went searching, moved to London

171

and eventually all the forces of fate and medical science put you in my overjoyed arms. But in your teenage years, as I tried to accentuate the positive you grew more frustrated with me, that I could not or would not appreciate the negative or see your point of view. You viewed what you already know, all those facts openly presented to you from a young age, as my story, not yours. You wanted to find out more about your unknown DNA and biological inheritance.

"Dear Sir or Madam,

I am one of the children that Doctor Robertson helped make. He planted a seed in my mum from a donor. Now it is my mum and me. My name is Natasha and I am 9½ and my mum's name is Carol and she is 40. We live in Edinburgh.

My reason for writing is to ask about the new law. I think you have guest it but if you have not it is about the idea of donors not being secret any more. I am curious about this. Right now children are asking there parents who is my donor and why. I asked my mum about him and she said write a letter and now I have worked up the courage to write it. Please change the law not just for me but all the children out there who are asking who is my donor.

Yours sincerly

Natasha Fox"

172

During those years, we had many long talks and many upsetting times. The subject of the donor was always there for you, deep down. Always. It would surface and disappear, come and go, reappear again and just as quickly disappear, crowded out in the midst of other normal teenage anxieties. But when you were tired or low, I could see the sadness in your eyes. These were very tough times indeed. It was really intense for you, and confusing for us both. I coped by loving you as hard as I could and by working hard. To your immense credit, despite everything, you worked equally hard at school, managing to focus on your school work and function outwardly, even though you could become increasingly upset and distressed, by not having information about your donor and feeling very alone in our tiny two person family in a world you saw populated by big happy families.

There was nothing I could do to change things. Besides, I had no regrets and I didn't want to wind the clock back, but I was equally determined to remain strong and positive. All we could do was be patient and wait, while I tried to provide as much love and support as I possibly could. From your perspective, I know I didn't always get it right. This story would not be honestly told if I did not record your sobs, the upset of a child who doesn't fully understand why she cannot know her donor and biological parent. I talked to you about the law on anonymity changing and you wrote to Dr Robertson.

While I wanted your unhappiness to be gone in an instant, I did not and could never for a minute regret my choice to bring you into the world as I did. The world is an immeasurably better place with you in it. I strived to support you, in your acceptance of the trials and tribulations that face us all in life and tried to encourage you to develop the tenacity and courage needed to face the particular loss you experience. Those teenage years within the circumstances of our family were very intense and rocky times, but with lots of love and care we have both survived and reached a better understanding.

In May 2006, I finally qualified as a solicitor. I boycotted the official admissions ceremony in favour of a party at the house for friends and family. It felt great to have overcome all the obstacles, and I was sure that my own battles would make me a better and more determined lawyer. You missed the party as you were away on a school trip to France as, at only fourteen, you were already a determined traveller.

And so we reached 2007, we had moved house and I had been promoted to associate level in the firm with the expected partnership not far around the corner. Exams had started at school and you did well, as predicted by all your teachers. While clever and studious, you had a wide circle of friends with a busy teenage social calendar. You found my approach over protective and you started to battle for your own independence. We are very different in many ways but we do share a very strong will. Lots of door slamming and shouting was not how I ever imagined motherhood and, for the first time, I started to feel very weary. I wanted to keep you safe from harm, while you wanted to get out into the world. It felt like a constant battle. Looking back, it was all normal teenage stuff, and I am so thankful now that you steered your own path with your own sense and increasing maturity. Meanwhile, you also developed a great sense of style and confidence and you looked stunning and eye catching. If you were in a good mood, you would offer to do my makeup and eyeliner to ensure that I too was presentable to the world.

In May 2007, there was another Scottish Parliament election and this time I decided to put my name forward for the Lothian Regional List. It seemed madness to stand in an unwinnable seat for a third time. I was ranked second on the Lothian regional list, just behind Lord George Foulkes. For some of us the old lord was a somewhat surprising result, as he had already retired from Westminster and was sitting very comfortably in the House of Lords, but he had been engineered by that not so clever party machine to the top of the list, even though he never wanted to be an MSP and preferred to remain

174

a lord in London. So, ranked as second on the regional list, once more I am a Labour Party candidate with little hope of election.

Don't ever believe anyone who tells you women don't put themselves forward for election, or that they just need the confidence and training to stand as candidates. Or that other great belief, that women should be elected on merit, while men are given a leg up at every turn. I could easily fill a large hall full of women in Scotland, bursting to the seams with merit who have been passed over by the party machine in favour of old lords and men with little discernible merit. One of the best lines I ever heard at conference was by a feminist Labour Party member, Rosina Macrae, *"Training? Don't talk to me about confidence building and training for women, some of us have had more training than the bloody Territorial Army and we still can't get a safe seat!"* Well said, sister. Boys without merit, somehow always manage to retain power. While women are worrying about endless training, to perfection and beyond, the mediocre men and sadly, some biddable women, are off being selected for safe seats. Be warned.

At a Hustings meeting during the 2007 Scottish Parliament election, I ended up on the same platform as my comrade brother, at a 'Stop the War Coalition' meeting. Throughout the meeting, Tony Blair was roundly and very angrily denounced as a war criminal. The audience was as hostile to a Labour Party candidate as it was possible to be. I was holding my own, I thought, explaining that not everyone in the Labour Party was a Blairite and many of us in the party had marched and opposed the Iraq war, until the heckling took a very nasty turn with pictures of dead Iraqi children held up by a row of people at the front. This was followed by heckling from a drunk guy, continually swearing, resulting in a very tense atmosphere. Just then, one of the other candidates intervened and said, *'Come on brothers and sisters, leave my wee sister alone, she might still be in the Labour Party but she is one of us.'* The audience sat up and only then realised the significance of us both being called 'Fox'. This family dynamic brought an interesting and more humorous dimension to the proceedings, although I was invited to defect and they continued to denounce the Labour Party, and all associated with it, as war criminals. Experience indeed! It made a great change for Colin to be fighting my battles and since then we forged an alliance, even if we still disagreed about the best strategies to affect real political change.

I left that meeting in 2007 knowing that the election was going to be very difficult for the Labour Party. We did indeed lose the election and a significant number of constituency seats. The SNP won by only one seat. As a result of the PR system the bold Lord George, for me the epitome of the right wing patriarchy, was elected from the list, one above me. For a minute it looked as though very unexpectedly I might get elected as Labour were doing so very badly in the constituency seats that more list seats looked like a distinct possibility. The election count was a complete fiasco and went on all night as the new electronic counting machines broke down. Thousands of people throughout Scotland were confused by the ballot papers and their votes were wasted with some ballot papers arriving from the islands, somehow ending up wet, having fallen in the sea. Some ballot papers floating in the sea could just be responsible for Scotland's subsequent march towards independence.

I was not elected, and in the great scheme of things I didn't really mind. I did mind a great deal that the party maneuvered an old Lord who had no commitment to being there, to the top of the list and into the Scottish Parliament to get paid a further salary while he spent half his week in the Lords in London. To this day, I refuse to be a Buddhist about this particular injustice. I spit in the eye of pundits who talk about the importance of women coming forward and standing for election. It might have been a personal disappointment for me, but was a much bigger disaster for the Scottish Labour Party (and there was worse to come as such "place men" and

176

"on message" candidates failed to inspire the nation next time around).

Still smarting from the indignity of being beaten, by the daft old Lord, I nevertheless put on a brave face, and shortly after the election in June 2007 attended a dinner in the Scottish Parliament. A number of journalists approached me, wanting to place bets about the odds of Lord Foulkes lasting the full four year term and me becoming an MSP after all. I smiled and declined to enter into such bets and speculation. I returned home fairly early after that dinner as Nana was through from Motherwell and was babysitting for you; by then a fifteen year old teenager.

I remember that night so well.

Chapter 19

I arrived home from the dinner at the Scottish Parliament feeling a bit deflated to find a brown envelope waiting for me. It contained an earlier attempt at writing this story, which I had sent a while before to a well-known name in Scottish publishing. The letter explained that it had taken some months to weigh up whether our story was a possible book, and with words of encouragement she advised me to rewrite and keep contacting publishers. A polite rejection I thought, they probably say that to everyone. Never mind. I remember holding this rejection letter in my hand, that evening, thinking about life, about politics, thinking wistfully about the past and about the future generally, about how difficult life can be when the phone rang.

It was after 11 pm.

At first I was very disoriented and confused, because I did not recognise the voice on the phone. All I could hear was an English, male voice, telling me that he had some sad news from Canada. He told me that Elliott had been involved in an accident and was on a life support machine. I heard the words 'motorbike', but I was thinking of Elliott, my godson, the baby and the four year old I looked after, the eleven year old of that last difficult holiday, mad on Harry Potter. What motorbike, I thought? Who had a motorbike? What has this to do with Elliott, as he had been saving for a car since he was sixteen? I could not compute the information I was hearing.

Seventeen year old Elliott had saved up for a car but, had instead, bought a motorbike, only two weeks before, and he was now on a life support machine. The doctors painted a bleak picture and said they wanted to do more tests, while they waited for his dad to fly out from England.

Elliott died the next day. 14th June 2007.

I could barely function. I could not be your mother. I could not be a lawyer. I could not get out of bed. I cried and cried. I sobbed until I was exhausted. I could only see the gorgeous baby and little boy that I loved and looked after before I was a mother myself, that smiling little boy who is in all our family photographs with you, being your big brother in those early years in London, helping me carry you in the car seat the day we left hospital. We were both so upset, but you tried to be so brave for me. You tried to help me, you made me some sweet tea and we both stayed at home. I was distraught at the injustice and unnecessary stupidity of it all and, absolutely, broken-hearted for Simone, after all the difficulties she had overcome. As you were going away on another school trip a few days later, I arranged to fly to Canada. I saw you off on the bus to France in a daze, even though I didn't want to let you out of my sight, I wanted to keep you close and safe.

By the time I arrived in Canada for the funeral, I was sad to find there was no body or coffin as Elliott had already been cremated, after a number of his organs were donated. The church service was so poignant and it felt as though everything was in slow motion. The service was full of shocked family, friends and school friends of Elliott's with a special reading from a First Nation's Elder who worked with Simone. This was followed by scattering seventeen year old Elliott's ashes on a Vancouver beach at English Bay. Simone was utterly devastated and clearly still in shock. I hugged her, but there was nothing to say, nothing anyone could say or do. Before I left for my flight home I tidied the house and cleaned the toilet. I did not know what else to do.

On the KLM flight back, I was seated next to a young couple who were already snogging the face off each other as the plane was taxiing along the runway. It would be a long and miserable flight, but I told myself I would be okay. As the plane soared above the clouds, my resolve disappeared. I started to cry, trying to contain and wipe away the tears. But when they started, I couldn't stop and I was soon engulfed by loud sobs. The young people beside me stopped kissing for a

179

minute, and looked at me very perplexed. Then a kind KLM stewardess appeared, and asked them to move seats. She sat down beside me, and held my hand for a while as I sobbed, the tears blinding the clouds as I poured out the grief for Simone and Elliott and what should have been. What might have been, had we all bought a house together in London all those years ago, what a wonderful mother Simone was to her only son and what a generous and kind friend she had been to us over the years. I have never cried so hard and hope I never experience such pain again, yet I experienced only a tiny fraction of Simone's grief. Only some strong sleeping pills and a brandy helped me to sleep the rest of the flight home. I will always remember the kindness of that flight attendant, who sat with me until I fell asleep and checked that I was okay.

As you were still away with the school, I returned to an empty house and worried myself sick until your safe return. Understandably, from then on, I worried about you. I was already an over protective mother, but after Elliott died I went through a terrible period of anxiety, when I would be gripped by a sudden fear that something terrible had happened to you. I needed to be able to contact you at all times and know exactly where you were and who you were with. This did not go down well with you, my sociable teenager, but we agreed that when you were out with friends at weekends you would keep in touch every few hours, texting just to let me know that you were okay.

Despite this agreement, one Saturday evening I had not heard from you, I had sent lots of texts and left increasingly frantic messages. It wasn't late but I tried your phone again, and this time it was answered by someone else. All I could hear was laughing voices in a noisy background. Instantly, I thought my worst fear had been realised, you had been abducted and someone had stolen your phone. I roared down the phone, shouting and swearing that if I did not get to speak to my daughter that very minute I was calling the police and they would trace the call and be there in the next five minutes.

The phone went dead and I was just about to call 999, when my phone rang. '*Hi Mum, it's me, I'm okay. I left my phone in my coat pocket, sorry, but some people in the bedroom heard it ring and answered it. They told me that you are going completely mental and calling the police. You are so embarrassing. Calm down and stop freaking out. I am just out at a party, be home soon.*' But by that stage I was so angry with you and so upset, that I got into the car and drove round to the party and made you come home early, much to your fury and embarrassment. Your teenage self often told me that I freaked out too much and was too overprotective. I remember, sounding just like my own mother, telling you just as often that, '*until you are a parent yourself, you simply cannot understand the depths of my fear and worry. You must keep in touch with me or you are not going out partying*'. We were poles apart; I was full of anxiety as you struggled for your freedom.

Before Elliott died, we had already booked our summer holiday and had planned to do a tour of Italy to help with your exams in art. Fortunately, when we went away we always had good holidays together, when it was only the two of us and we had lots to do and see. We were flying to Rome, then taking a train to Florence, visiting Pisa, then on to Venice. So in July 2007, we had a very cultural holiday discovering Renaissance Italy. It was only a few weeks after Elliott's funeral and I remember laying on the beach at the Lido in Venice, wondering how the world could be so beautiful and yet life could be so unfair and so tragic, that Elliott was not partying somewhere in Canada. I kept telling myself that he was dead, but this wee boy kept smiling right back at me telling me not to be so stupid, he was at home watching the Little Mermaid video and he still didn't like that horrible purple lady.

Following the funeral in Canada, Elliott's grandmother organised an English service for family and friends in August 2007. I wrote an obituary for the 'Other Lives' section of The Guardian, as I knew that lots of our previous social work friends in London would see it. I kept checking and when it wasn't printed, I contacted them. I got a brief e-mail back telling me that unfortunately what I had written did not fit with their house style. House style? House bloody style? I fired off an immediate infuriated reply telling the editor pointedly that a seventeen year old boy, an only child, being killed in a motorbike accident in Canada did not fit with anyone's house style, did not fit with any cosmic plan and the very least he could do as a fellow human being was to print a few short sad sentences for the sake of the family. Elliott's obituary was published in the 'Other Lives' section of The Guardian on 23rd July 2007.

We gathered in August 2007 in the same small English church in Dorset, where Elliott had been christened when he was eighteen months and I had stood as his godmother when I was four months pregnant with you. As we looked down at the small, simple, gravestone 'Elliott Lyall Harty, 15.4.1990 – 14.6.2007', our lives in London felt like another world away, full of possibilities with a smiling and energetic wee boy and my baby in my arms.

I have not yet properly dealt with this grief. Perhaps I never will. I do not feel that I have the right. I do not feel I have the right to feel this sad, or, this angry. Simone has every right to rage against the world. My confused feelings and thoughts are always about a baby, a wee boy I loved and looked after in London. I like to pretend he is still growing up in Canada and I will meet him one day as a healthy young man. To lose a child is devastating, to lose your only child is unimaginable and to keep our children safe is the keenest and yet most elusive of all our responsibilities as parents. Elliott was in some ways a typical teenage boy, yet he was also fluent in French, a gifted musician and had a great flare for cooking. Simone gave her son the best life she could. One silly teenage mistake, one reckless act, one night cost him his life. I have a box full of photographs and letters and the last polite 'thank you' note from Elliott.

Dear Carol and Natasha,

Thank you very much for the £50 you gave me for my birthday. It was very generous of you. I've gone off cars as I get my motorcycle license on June 2nd. They're alot faster and environmentally friendly! I went to Whistler for the weekend with some mates for the my birthday weekend. It was really good and I saw Damien and Stephen Marley in Concert for free. Hope your both well. Lots of love

Elliott

He qualified with his motorcycle license on 2nd June 2007, exactly fifteen years to the day when he came to the hospital as a two year old to visit you on the day you were born. Yet Elliott died only two weeks after getting his license at only seventeen, on 14th June 2007. A tragic loss, which has caused such grief for so many people scattered around the world.

Chapter 20

The rest of 2007 passed in a haze of work and the usual routine and demands of getting through each day. Our lives were focused on school and exams, and our battles of your early teenage years, eased off. I had been promoted again to the position of Head of Equality, but things were not as they should have been within the law firm and the retirement of my mentor, the senior partner in Edinburgh, made things worse. The tensions between the external image and the internal reality became unbearable for me.

There is no doubt that Elliott's death influenced my decision to leave that law firm in 2008. Death gives you a very different perspective on life. Despite my previous struggles (or perhaps more accurately probably *because* of all my previous struggles and battles), I felt strongly that life was too short to settle for less, even though it would have been so much easier to sit in my room with my head down and accept my lot, satisfied that I had achieved a certain degree of mid-ranking success. But as Head of Equality. I could not remain in a law firm which, at that time, had not made a woman a partner in ten years. Much more than that I cannot explain, except to borrow a few good lines from Hilary Mantel, the feminist author and Booker prize winner who studied law. She writes in her memoir, "*A few brave women from unhelpful backgrounds had crashed the system. Some people have forgotten, or never known, why we needed the feminist movement so badly. This is why: so that some talentless prat in a nylon shirt couldn't patronise you.*"

Well said, Hilary.

So I left, not knowing exactly what was going to happen next. I arranged to work for a few months as a volunteer in the Ethnic Minority Law Centre in Edinburgh. I sent my CV to Stefan Cross, a solicitor in Newcastle specialising in equal pay cases. He was pleased to offer me a job and we agreed that I would start on 1st October 2008. It hadn't been part of any sensible plan to live in Edinburgh and work in Newcastle but it was a challenging and ideal opportunity, and so I agreed to a cross border commute, while taking over responsibility for 10,000 equal pay claims already lodged within the Scottish Employment Tribunal.

As I was between jobs, with more time on my hands than I ever expected, we decided to have an extended six week holiday travelling across America. Putting everything behind us, we had an absolute ball visiting thirteen cities, knowing that I had a new job to return to in October. We flew first to Vancouver and picked up Simone who was still lost in acute grief one year later, but managed somehow to spend some time with us in Seattle, San Francisco and Los Angeles. You and I then flew on to Chicago, then we travelled down the East Coast of America by Amtrak. Our six week American trip was one of our first great mother and daughter adventures.

At only sixteen, your intelligence, maturity, adventurous spirit and keen interest in history often left me astounded. On each and every visit to a museum or historical site, you read every detail of the guide, keen to learn all the historical facts, while I was already out the other end browsing in the gift shop, looking for tasteful souvenirs. You were also a well-rounded typical teenager, so as well as the museums, galleries and sites, we visited almost every single Abercrombie and Fitch shop in North America. As ever the over protective mother, I was shocked by the half-naked young men parading about these stores, so you would sit me gently in a corner in a large brown leather chair while you spent endless hours in the dressing rooms. It is amazing the kind of feminist thinking time you can have in shops, when your teenage daughter is fashion mad. While spending one such afternoon sitting in the corner, I got a call on my mobile from the anti-fraud department of my bank to alert me to the fact that my credit card had been used extensively across North America.

Travelling and having adventures together has been a

wonderful aspect of your later teenage years. After America, the following year in 2009, when you were studying Advanced Higher Moral and Religious Philosophy, we went on a three week trip to Ancient China to visit Buddhist temples and the Great Wall. It is such a wonderful feeling to take you to new places and share in your excitement and interest in learning more about the world. You have an insatiable appetite for new places and adventure which I try to support, even though I want to hold your hand, keep you close and lead you safely through life. Even at sixteen, I began to realise that you had to be allowed to find your own way, although balancing your spirit of adventure with my level of anxiety has never been easy. You might find out for yourself one day how hard it is to let children go and allow them freedom to explore the world.

Chapter 21

On 1ˢᵗ October 2008, I began my cross border commute when my alarm went off at 5:30 am. I needed to be out of the house by 6:30 to make the train to Newcastle, aiming to get to the office outside the city centre for 9. I had booked the return ticket on the 5:40 pm train and so would get home by 7:30. So my long days of fighting for equal pay began.

Fortunately, I did not need to travel south every day as there were often tribunal hearings in Glasgow or Edinburgh. I could also work remotely and tried to be as flexible as possible, while supporting you at school with your next set of exams. Doing well, your focus was on university and there was a great deal of discussion about a gap year, which I wanted you to arrange after university but which you persisted in researching and making plans for after the last year at school. For the moment, your focus was on finishing school and my professional focus shifted to the challenge of mass litigation and the world of equal pay.

It did come as something of a surprise that in 2008, there were over ten thousand equal pay claims at tribunals on behalf of low paid female council workers throughout Scotland. This entrenched pay inequality was the result of historical bonus payments made to groups of male workers such as refuse collectors, road sweepers and gardeners, but not paid to women on the same pay grade who worked as cleaners, carers or catering assistants. In the late eighties, due to national government pay restraint, the local government unions negotiated local arrangements to ensure productivity payments and other bonuses. This was perfectly lawful and the bonuses could have been justified, if they were genuinely related to productivity. However, no attempts were made to negotiate the same higher earnings for female workers and, worse still, any productivity element of the male bonus payments soon fell away with the extra payments to the men being guaranteed for turning up. Given the gender segregation of the workforce, the women remained largely ignorant of the extra payments being made to men on the same grade for just turning up in the morning. Some men were even paid a bonus when off on the sick or away at trade union meetings. The difference in pay was not just a few pence here and there. In most cases, it was as much as 50% of basic salary, and in some outrageous cases more than 100% or even 150%.

Of course, the women knew little or nothing about this. The employers and the unions, who had negotiated these extra payments only for their male members, knew exactly what was going on and they knew that the additional payments to male workers were unjustified. The unions knew for years that the women had viable equal pay claims. But there was a deliberate conspiracy of silence. Attempts were made to renegotiate new collective agreements, but neither the employers nor the unions would risk industrial action by withdrawing the additional payments to the men, and could not go public as they would then alert the women to the pay inequality. In 1997, the employers' organisation in Scotland, COSLA, reached agreement with the unions that they would not support *any* legal cases for the women. In 1999 a new collective agreement was struck, but the unions and the employers dragged their feet once more and nothing changed. Meanwhile, the women were still unaware that their male counterparts on the same pay grade were being paid at least 50% more, and no one in their union was telling them. Female union members paid subscriptions for years, but were kept in the dark. When some women did find out, because they were married to or lived beside refuse collectors or gardeners, their union failed to support a legal challenge and in some cases lied to them that there was no inequality in pay.

This scandal and complacency continued for years and could have dragged on indefinitely, but for the intervention of Stefan Cross. Not only did he publicise the issue, he wholly upset the apple cart by encouraging women to lodge legal complaints at the Employment Tribunal operating on a no win no fee basis. The first Scottish claims were lodged in August 2005, and only then did the unions have to follow suit when litigation had forced their hand and challenged the role of the unions in maintaining this pay discrimination. The unions, in a spectacularly hypocritical example of "shoot the messenger", hated Stefan's guts with such an irrational passion, not only because he is English but because he blew the whistle on the all-too-cosy relationship between the employers and the unions, which betrayed the rights of their female members for years. Worst still, he became seriously rich in the process. This anger towards lawyers continues while the unions wholly fail to examine their own record in maintaining pay inequality and failing to support their female members over decades while deducting union subs from their wages. For feminists in the labour and trade union movement, this remains a scandal which the male hierarchy refuse to face. It is another *Made in Dagenham* tale only forty years later.

Fully aware of this furore and the increasing numbers of claims at the tribunal, I had sent my CV to Newcastle in 2008 to see if I could help win equal pay cases for thousands of low paid women in Scotland. My focus was always upon the women and for me it was feminism in action, delivering real money to many thousands of real low paid women. Reasonable people might view this as a laudable objective, but the rancour which persists in Scotland resulted for a time in me becoming persona non-grata in my previous trade union and Labour Party circles. This is fairly easily explained as the very same trade union officials who negotiated the unlawful bonus payments for male union members while ignoring the women, are also stalwarts of the Labour Party or councillors or both. Some of the councillors mired in this scandal became MPs and MSPs. Even so, it is difficult to accept when previous friends and comrades walk on the other side of the street and cannot look me in the eye.

Scotland is a very small country and so the same people can

exercise power, especially in the West of Scotland, in a very unhealthy and incestuous fashion, where little space is left for any accountability or integrity. While condemning others, few within the trade union movement have yet examined their own conscience, and their continued denial is focused upon hatred of one lawyer who enabled women to stand up for their rights and became personally very successful while doing so. He triumphantly drives a red Ferrari around the streets of Newcastle.

From 2008, the daily reality of fighting these equal pay cases was gruelling, such was the general hostility of the employers, the unions and the legal establishment. The legal preparation requires a forensic analysis of the jobs undertaken by the male comparators and the female claimants. I could now easily appear on Mastermind with my specialist subject, *'Refuse Drivers Bonus Earnings'*. I also have a very detailed knowledge of the work of our thousands of female claimants, who may have several part-time jobs to fit around childcare and domestic responsibilities. For example, we had a long running case, a home carer, who did back to back shifts looking after the elderly and vulnerable in their homes. She was offered £2,500 in settlement of her equal pay claim. She was due nearer £54,000. In Glasgow, it became clear that the council paid more to male gardeners to look after the flower beds in the parks than they paid to women to look after the elderly. Then the council paid huge amounts of tax payers' money to corporate lawyers to try to defend the indefensible. These equal pay cases make my feminist blood boil. Sadly, far too many of our claimants have died as we pursue their legal cases in the face of determined opposition. Scottish councils instructed highly paid barristers to make tired legal arguments which were bound to fail. Worse still, the tribunal system affords them a modicum of respect that somehow we are all just doing our job as professional people. It is a scandal yet to be fully unveiled, but when it is I will be glad to have been on the side of the low paid women.

The Employment Tribunal System has also struggled to cope with thousands of cases. Fortunately, a number of council areas eventually reached out of court settlements, which gave some women life changing amounts of compensation and back pay. We have received hundreds of 'Thank You' cards, which are my pride and joy. The humour, determination and resilience of the women remind me so much of the Glasgow women I first met all those years ago in the Broomielaw Hostel. During one tribunal hearing, when one of our home helps was giving evidence, the clever lawyer on the other side in cross examination asked her about bonus payments. *'Is there really any way your employer could design a bonus scheme for your job?'* Quick as a flash she replied:

'Well, son, I should think so, they put a man on the moon after all.'

I wanted to bound over the witness table and give her a hug. He sat down, red faced and admitted defeat.

She won that case for her and thousands of others.

Chapter 22

Following the success of the equal pay cases and based on my experience to date, I received my accreditation as a specialist in discrimination law by the Law Society of Scotland in June 2009. In order to bring my cross border commute to an end, we finally opened a new law firm in Edinburgh in January 2010. Hurrah.

However, the sheer effort of setting up the new firm complying with the regulations of the Law Society of England and Wales and the Law Society of Scotland, as well as finding fully accessible office premises was daunting. The new firm also had to hit the ground running as all the existing Scottish cases and bulging filing cabinets were delivered from Newcastle. I soon found myself in charge of everything, as Stefan also had the Newcastle office to run. At the beginning of 2010, there was hardly time to draw breath between interviewing for staff, organising the office, tribunal hearings and in the midst of all that rolling out another major settlement. I was much too busy to feel any sense of excitement that I had achieved my goal to be a recognised Equality Lawyer, and that somehow quite beyond the realms of any of my five year plans or previous ambitions, I was the director of my own law firm.

Besides which, our clients always keep my feet firmly on the ground. In Glasgow we represented over four thousand five hundred women and as news of the settlement spread, it seemed like all of our clients were on the phone in the space of a week, all largely with the same questions, '*Haw, hen, when am I getting my money*?' We all did our best to progress settlements and everyone in the office worked extremely hard. I regularly took files home with me and worked until 1 am or 2 am in the morning with memories of the law degree and studying ten years before in my mind. The sheer scale of mass litigation, as well as the demands of the individual clients, who understandably want lawyers to pay attention to their individual case, can be immensely difficult to manage. I worked late in the office, even later at home and on at least one occasion decided not to go home and worked through the night. All of a sudden my life was overtaken by equal pay and the responsibility of running a small business.

At the same time, you were completing your sixth year at school, once again doing well in Advanced Higher exams. You wanted to study History and Politics and applied for places at Edinburgh University, Glasgow and Newcastle. Although you accepted your place at Edinburgh University, you made it clear that you had applied to start in September 2011, as you were determined to have your much longed for gap year. You also made it clear that you wanted to go to Edinburgh University, but did not want to stay at home. One thing at a time, I thought.

Without any help, or I have to admit much initial support from me, you went ahead and planned your gap year. When you told me that this included spending four months as a teaching assistant in a primary school in Kenya, I thought I was going to have to blow into a brown paper bag to regulate my breathing. I heard myself saying, '*You are only eighteen, you are not going to Africa'*, to which you instantly replied, *'that is so unfair, you went to Sudan'*. '*Yes but I was twenty-five and a qualified social worker, you are still at school.*' These 'so unfair' conversations went on for several months. I decided not to overplay my hand with too much vehement opposition, hoping you would change your mind and want to go to university at the same time as all of your friends. I should have known better.

Your determination grew and plans became flight times and meetings with Africa Venture. I finally relented and it was all confirmed that you would fly to Nairobi at the beginning of September 2010. You were so excited, and I was just as equally terrified at the thought of you being so far away for so long. It seemed to me that one minute we were in the Early Learning Centre playing with Duplo people and the next you

193

were waving goodbye as you decided to go off to Africa. I tried not to think about it. I was petrified and letting you go was harder than I can ever explain.

In June 2010, you turned eighteen. Not long after your birthday and the school prom, you produced the HFEA forms which you had been waiting to fill out since you were thirteen. You could now officially register with the HFEA and make an application to find out non-identifiable details of the donor and whether you had any half siblings. We talked this all through very carefully and had to complete official forms sending passports and birth certificates to the HFEA. I had been deliberately holding you back throughout your teenage years until you were ready to take this step and now that you had arrived at the right age, I wanted to temper your expectations.

I reminded you all about the twenty-nine cycles of fertility treatment, which meant that it was unlikely there would be any siblings and that despite the change in the law in 2005, your donor retained the right to remain anonymous. We posted the letter to the HFEA recorded delivery and waited patiently for a response. We agreed that if any special delivery letter arrived for you, or for me, with the HFEA stamp we would open it together. This was not, however, a legally binding or enforceable contract.

Two weeks later, sitting at my desk in the office, immersed in work, my mobile rang and your excited voice said, *'I have four siblings, two boys and two girls, all born in 1992 and 1993.'* You were surprised and very happy. I was stunned. I didn't want to spoil your excitement by reminding you about our agreement to open the HFEA letter together when I got home. I reassured you that I was happy for you, and would talk to you all about it as soon as I finished work. I had genuinely thought there was no chance of any other offspring. As I contemplated this surprise development, it hit me that someone else, somewhere else, had had my twins. I was pleased about the possibilities this opened up for you, but my own feelings and thoughts were in turmoil. I had to try especially hard to focus on the struggle for equal pay that afternoon.

When I got home, we had a long talk. We read the letter carefully, reviewing the details of the donor and the fact that your name was now on a voluntary register to be able to make contact with your half siblings. Given the dates of birth of the boy and girl in 1992 and another boy and girl in 1993, I explained that you were probably the first to reach eighteen and you would need to wait until they were old enough to request information from the HFEA. It also depended, I reminded you, on whether they had been told openly, as you had about their assisted conception.

Then our attention turned to the donor. We already had my medical records and knew the brief details recorded by the HFEA ,so there was nothing new there. All those years ago, I had been surprised to find out that he was a theatre director/ manager with an interest in the Arts, as most people assume medical students are the main source of donations. From the dates of the last treatment and the ten year use by dates in 2001, he must have donated in London in 1991. *'How difficult can it be to find a theatre director in London? Can we hire a private detective?'* you said. *'No, we can't',* I insisted, *'it will cost a fortune and they would have nothing more than we have to go on right now.'* I explained to you that due to the timing of the original HFEA legislation in 1991 and the recent 2005 change in the law, it is possible for the donor to re-register and agree to remove his anonymity. So we agreed that the best way forward was to try to raise awareness, and if possible find out more information ourselves.

We then agreed that as you were about to go to Kenya and were only just eighteen, you needed to take this journey one stage at a time. We made a pact that night that I would stop putting the brakes on and support you in your quest to know the identity of your donor and, if possible, make contact with your biological siblings.

The months when you were away in Kenya were awful. I felt bereft. I lived in a constant state of anxiety, losing myself in work to get me through the day but I worried all the time. You were only able to keep in touch intermittently and when you did contact me, it tended to be because you had a problem with money or you were planning another trip with fellow volunteers. This Africa experience involved teaching in the primary school and then squeezing in trips to other places like Uganda and Zanzibar. My nerves were shattered. Yet your sense of adventure at eighteen was undaunted by any sense of danger, even though you told me that you had to keep bribing local police who stopped the buses and demanded money if you wanted to get anywhere safely. Several times, after I put the phone down, I wanted to fly immediately to Kenya to bring you home and keep you safe under my roof.

The internet is a terrible invention for worried parents in the middle of the night, when a quick Google search reveals stories of adventures gone wrong. One young woman on the same venture as yours a few years before was killed by a crocodile. Jesus. My normal tendency to worry went into

196

overdrive and my fears were only contained by focusing on work. You told me that I was complaining too much, '*you have to let me live my own life.*' From my perspective, shouldering the sole responsibility of bringing you into the world and looking after you for eighteen years could not be so easily shrugged off.

Chapter 23

While you were away, I focused upon the next milestone in my life, becoming fifty on 11.1.11. We agreed that I would book a cruise and that you would come with me for my fiftieth birthday. '*It will be awful,*' you said, '*full of old people and very boring, but I will do it for you.*' So I spent the rest of my free time during your gap year searching the internet for an affordable cruise which fitted in with your return home and my birthday. I finally settled upon a Thomson's cruise flying first to Cuba, then cruising around the Caribbean. Bliss. The tickets duly arrived, made into a personalised little book with my name on it. I opened it, excited to read all about the different ports of call we were due to visit, only to find myself staring directly at the smiling face of Elliott's father. Bizarre. By now an aging male model, I recognised him straight away, even though I had only seen him twice before, once at Highbury and Islington Court and again in Canada at Elliott's funeral. These moments in life are just too uncanny.

In 2010, Christmas arrived with incredible snow storms which brought the country to a standstill and closed all the airports. It looked like you were going to be stranded in Kenya. Fortunately, you managed to get the last flight out to Heathrow and following a number of panic calls, telling me that you were stranded in London, I arranged to collect you from your friend's house in Yorkshire. Due to complicated directions, we finally managed to meet up again in a car park off the A1 motorway services in the midst of snow and ice. Hugging you again, home safe and well after four months in Africa, was the greatest feeling on earth. You are always so embarrassed when I cry.

Contrary to your predictions, we then had a great time on the cruise and it was so lovely to spend time together again. When we came home you had planned the remainder of your gap year, as you had successfully applied for an unpaid internship three days a week with Amnesty International in London, spending the other two days helping Katy Clark MP at the House of Commons. In February, we travelled down to London together and you settled into the smallest bedsit possible in Clapham, South London. I came back on the train later the same night, overnight on the sleeper. As I lay there, rocking from side to side kept awake by the noise as the train sped north, I was miserable that you were alone in London. Then I thought back to all the train journeys I had made from Scotland to London, Brighton and Eastbourne to bring you into this world. During that long journey back to Scotland, it dawned on me that it was time to let you go and my role was now to give you all possible support with your future plans. At eighteen you had already shown such guts and a mature, self-assured attitude to life.

The upside was the peace and quiet, and the complete tidiness of the house in your absence. I learned to appreciate my order and tranquillity after a hard day at the office and also realised that I needed to embrace much more positively your plans to move out and to go to university. After all, it was inevitable that you wanted to move out and become independent.

During that gap year in 2011, this story remained half told and was hidden away amongst all my papers and files. Occasionally, I would think about the advice I had received in 2007, the day before Elliott died, to keep going and to rewrite. Grief stopped me. Four years later, I was slowly learning to let go of that grief and at the same time I was learning to let go of you, to allow you to grow up and find your own direction.

My mind turned to the past. Somehow, it all just felt less painful than before. Something had shifted. So I decided that I should use my new found time wisely and write down my journey from the exploding ovaries towards motherhood. Just like when I decided to become an unconventional mother, I had no idea where to start. How do you go about writing a book?

How does a jumble of ideas and life experiences become a story that means anything to anyone else?

Mulling things over in my head one weekend, I came across an advert in the Sunday Times for a very interesting twelve week course on 'Life Writing with Gillian Slovo' run by Faber and Faber in London. *'Why are all these great courses always in London?'* I thought to myself, but I e-mailed for further details anyway. The course looked so interesting, weekly from 7-9 pm on Monday evenings and over one weekend, with visiting authors and writing exercises. The pull of the authors and of Gillian Slovo translated my musings about *'How would I find the time?'* into more definite plans. It would just about be possible, if I could contain the struggle for equal pay for a few hours, work on the train down to London on Monday afternoons and return on the sleeper so that I could be in the office the next day. Thus, from October to December 2011, this working class girl from Motherwell found herself having interesting Monday evenings in Bloomsbury. It was a stroke of life affirming madness which enabled me to step out of my demanding Edinburgh lawyer's life and step into a whole new dimension, populated as it was by intellectual writers and would-be authors. There are whole areas of life which some lucky people can inhabit comfortably, which are such unknown territory to others. By chance, I met the most fascinating group of twelve people with diverse backgrounds and interesting stories.

Admittedly, some of that group were more interested in talking about writing than producing a paragraph, but having paid my money and with travelling to London on a weekly basis, I wanted to take the course seriously. The writing exercises were challenging, but the most daunting aspect of the course for me was listening to the sometimes harrowing experiences of child abuse, suicide and unhappiness; sadly unavoidable dark moments of the human condition. I felt confused, as I wanted to write our story for you but, above all, I wanted to make it positive and life affirming.

My own dark and lighter moments have passed so quickly during the last three decades covered by this story. On the course we read such a lot of books that I now have a small library of biographies and memoirs. Doing the research over the past few years has been eye opening with permission to read, think and ponder. I learned that no one needs to write a cradle-to-grave history about all the ups and downs of life. So, I decided to write about my (in)fertile years, about the means of reproduction. In her recent memoir, Jeanette Winterston assertively decided not to cover twenty-five years of her life. So I equally assertively have left out some chapters and some people. Some things I can't write about in detail for legal reasons. I deleted a much longer chapter on my financial struggles which I have managed, if I don't say so myself, with such fantastic aplomb. I love the quote from Oscar Wilde: *"People who live within their means, lack imagination."*

A suggestion was made that I should have a running total of the cost of all the fertility treatment at the end of each chapter, so I looked through all my papers and every receipt that I have kept in a large file for you. But it has proved a step too far. I will leave that to someone else, after I'm long gone. The answer to you and the curious reader is many, many thousands of pounds which was mostly begged and borrowed, then slowly paid off. Most people use their Marks and Spencer's card for posh food or sensible pants, but I found it worked just as well for trying to make babies. Of course, it wasn't sensible and I often had to move to the land of the minimum payment, but being sensible or conventional has clearly never been my thing.

Over the years, I have taken a relatively guilt free and creative approach to money, as I have enthusiastically embraced my dear flexible friends, as and when required, acquiring lots of good debt. Not so much bad debt really, and always another five year plan in the background. So far, so good, and the rest, if it ever needs to be unearthed, can be done later, much later when I am too old to care.

Besides which, if we all stopped to think about the cost of having children, the world would surely grind to a halt in an instant. I say, it is not common sense nor good financial planning that keeps the world turning, but us mothers, who take a leap of faith on the next generation. Having become a single mother against the odds, I just refused to become miserable about what I didn't have, even though I still want to go back now to Stoke Newington Church Street to buy those expensive cheeses and a few wholly unnecessary scented candles.

In 2012, spending a bit more money and with a very large dollop of irony (given their previous editorial in 1991 which negatively affected my life), I attended another writing weekend master class in London at the Guardian, run by Frances Wilson, a fantastic, enthusiastic, teacher and writer. This involved more fascinating authors, interesting people and a realisation that many people, from many walks of life enjoy middle class pastimes, spending money on writing courses. And there I was, amongst it all.

On top of reading loads of books, as an aspiring writer, I also made my yearly homage to the Edinburgh International Book Festival, and attended the Aye Write Festival in Glasgow. Listening to Jeanette Winterston, Jackie Kay and Janice Galloway, inspired me to keep going with this story, even though sitting alone in front of a keyboard, looking out of the window, can feel like such a questionable enterprise. But what has really spurred me on to finally finish my tale of positive and determined motherhood, was attending an event at the Edinburgh Book Festival with Rachel Cusk.

Rachel delivered a very raw and upsetting reading from her memoir about her separation and divorce, the essence of which was that as a feminist she had failed as a wife and a mother, that it was all just too hard. Her conclusion, thrown open to the audience for further discussion, was that modern mothers are utterly bewildered, full of angst and absolutely guilt ridden that we cannot provide our children with an ideal family life, while also pursuing a fulfilling career. Her message was that it all ends in tears as it had for her, despite her best efforts. Her thesis was that "having it all" has proved impossible. She cast such a very sad figure, sitting there on the platform, in a tent full of avid readers and no doubt a fair few feminists, as though she was in mourning for her feminist beliefs. To me, she seemed more in need of a good feed and a lie down than an exhausting and emotional book tour. While trying to remain sympathetic to a fragile woman in a highly vulnerable and nervous state, my blood boiled at hearing yet another treatise on how "having it all" is too hard, how women should all retreat to the safer image of a modern Stepford wife, albeit now tied to a more expensive kitchen with marble work surfaces, a Belfast sink and an open plan living area so that we can help with the children's homework while drizzling olive oil over the tomato and mozzarella salad. That'll be the day, I thought, over my dead body. I just will not have it.

To my mind, doubt about whether you will manage to get to the end of the week or the end of the month, juggling work, family and finances, is just not the same as guilt. Guilt implies that mothers have done something wrong, that we have let people down by our own selfish need to have a life. Yet we are motivated by our desire to do our best, and it is most often only our own needs that are sacrificed in the process. As women, we have to seize control and not give away our power to direct our own lives and define our own aspirations. I may not speak for all women and my experience of motherhood has certainly been unconventional, but I suspect more women, mothers with and without partners, share my determination to do our very best by our kids. Why do we need to be silenced and accept just quiet satisfaction from our efforts and hard work? Why can't we shout from the roof tops of the joy we experience in motherhood and raising our children? We need to drown out those guilty and anguished voices and use our energies more wisely to change our laws and our workplaces to ensure working parents have greater support.

When it came to the questions at the book festival I raised my hand and tried to temper my contribution with a little humour. '*As a working mother I am not in the least bit bewildered or guilt ridden, and I don't give a toss about what other people think, as I know that every day I try to do my very best,*' adding that I just wished mothers offered each other positive support instead of all the endless handwringing. The audience clapped enthusiastically and a large number of women came up to me in the book signing queue later, saying they felt the same but didn't have the guts to say it out loud, as we are all supposed to feel so guilty. Well to hell with that, why are we allowing ourselves to be silenced with only one version of modern motherhood allowed on the airwaves?

I don't understand why mothers allow others to deny the reality of our own lived experience. Being your mother has been wonderful. All this utter nonsense about aiming for the *ideal*, the ideal family and the ideal job, making it all work smoothly every day of every week is just such a complete con. There are thousands, if not millions, of working mothers in this country who get to the end of each week, pour themselves a glass of wine feeling satisfied that they have manoeuvred around or through the obstacles placed in their path to give their kids the best future they can. I know because I am one of them, and I could also fill a large tent in Edinburgh any day of the week with hard working mothers who have a positive self regard about doing their very best for their children. Our anger should be focused upon the boss or bad employer, those complete arses of male (and sadly some female) bosses who, having never spent a nanosecond of their own time changing a nappy, deny requests for flexible working. Or that infuriating male mindset with such sympathy for a colleague's drunken injury and time off after a rugby game or stag weekend, but complete lack of any empathy when our children are ill and we need a few days off. I will gladly continue to rage against the patriarchy, in all its forms, every day of every week. When I have come up against it face to face, and I have often done so, I do something about it. We have laws in this country to protect women from these kind of double standards and discrimination, but we have to take ourselves seriously first. I just can't understand why other women are not angrier too.

You have come to feminism in your own way and your own time. As you have now passed your twenty-first birthday, you are trying to find your future path which at the moment is windy and uncertain as you question the world around you. If you embrace your beliefs with passion they will give you great strength. But you also have to devise survival mechanisms to keep yourself sane and learn to direct your anger productively. My advice is to recognise the patriarchy in all its guises and learn to protect yourself. You must also learn to look after yourself. I want you to know that the arguments you will hear about "having it all" and how it is all too hard are only half the truth. Of course it is hard, especially when you swim against the tide, and it can be exhausting and damaging for some women, but to be forewarned is to be forearmed. It is up to you to develop resilience and to determine your own destiny and make your own choices. And you will get all the help and support you need from me. An intelligent woman has many enemies, but believing in yourself and your ability to determine your own destiny will enable you to overcome the daily frustrations of being patronised by people who lack the courage of their convictions.

What often saddens me is the acquiescence of some professional women in their own oppression, repeatedly passed over for promotion, refused part-time work, sacked for becoming pregnant. It happens every week, yet even those women with the professional and financial means to do something about it, such as lawyers, still live in a deluded world, somehow believing that smiling and working hard will inevitably lead to a fair outcome. It's when that professional disillusionment sets in, when it is so hard to be treated with respect and be taken seriously as an equal in the workplace, because you have to leave at a particular time to collect children, that we bear the brunt of our own frustrations. We need to turn those frustrations outwards and into action. We all know tales of the men who stay in the office late to gather brownie points, even though they are often slumped over their desk having a snooze, surfing the net or chatting about football.

I cannot abide the softly, softly post-feminist, counter propaganda that we now endure, that it is all just too difficult and women cannot possibly have it all. Bullshit. I will not stay silent when I witness injustice and inequality. To hell with Melanie Phillips and her ilk, and over my dead body will anyone take your hard won rights away or narrow your horizons.

I can't believe I still have to protest this shit...?

But you also need to be vigilant.

When I try to read books by younger feminists such as Caitlin Moran, I truly despair. When did feminism become stand-up comedy? She tries so hard to get a laugh while mentioning the F word, almost apologising for being serious. Yet Caitlin really doesn't know she is born, she barely acknowledges the fights and struggles of previous generations. Instead she turns feminism into fashionista stuff, high heels and ladette culture. The story of her dog eating the used sanitary towel was all too much for me. There is no point falling out with younger feminists, but I have not campaigned during my forty years of feminism so that young women can walk about the streets half- dressed and tottering about on bloody stupid shoes. While you are marching for the right to wear short skirts and boob tubes, powerful men are once again colonising your ovaries and wombs determining when and how you will have babies. Bishops and politicians are once more deciding how many weeks you have to consider an abortion, with a free vote for male politicians and yet no free vote of conscience for any woman to determine when or if she wants to be a mother. If you can't control your own body, you can't control hellish much in your life. If only men would either butt out of this debate entirely or approach the subject of abortion and reproduction with much more humility. If only young women like you could truly understand the battles of your foremothers, fought to give you the important choices you have in life. I want you to cherish and value the opportunities ahead of you.

Please persuade your younger sisters, less focus on the ladette culture and daft shoes, more on tackling the patriarchy head on by demanding control of your own reproduction. I have attached a list of feminist books that have sat on my bookshelves for years. Great feminist thinkers and writers who inspired my generation have passed away, but their books and ideas are so important, we cannot allow their struggles and personal sacrifices to be in vain. It is a downright criminal lie that women have achieved equality. If we do not guard our rights they will subtly, or not so subtly, be rolled back and your generation will have fewer choices and less control over your lives.

I read with huge trepidation in the Scottish newspapers that the Bishop of Motherwell, in my hometown, has likened abortion clinics to Auschwitz, following a protest outside the very same BPAS clinic I attended in Brighton all those years ago. As feminists, we need to treasure our hard won rights to control our own lives. You always hear those bishops argue that abortion involves two lives, not one. Not, I loudly respond, when you have to look down a microscope to see one life while the needs of the other, of the woman in front of you, are staring you in the face.

You are living in a world where doctors in Ireland allowed a woman, Savita Halappanavar, to die unnecessarily rather than heed her pleas for a termination, where a brave teenage girl Malala was shot in the head for campaigning for education, where women in Egypt are being harassed and forced out of a popular political uprising and where a young medical student in India died after being gang raped and thrown from a public bus. Here in Scotland, we still have Women's Aid Refuges in every town and we are still fighting thousands of equal pay cases. Post bloody feminism? I don't bloody think so, not for a minute.

It is tragic, and so disheartening, that this is the world you inherit after forty years of your mother's and others' feminist struggles. You have every right to be angry. I am so proud that you are now weighing up for yourself what kind of feminist you are, what feminism means to you and finding your own voice. You told me how uncomfortable you are when other students use the C word as you find it offensive not empowering, and that you felt so concerned when another student made a placard which said, *I've had five abortions, so what*? You don't want to use shock tactics or be intimidating. Instead, you want to use your passion and anger to campaign and engage in intellectual arguments and debate. I hope you manage but it is also okay to be angry, you can't always remain calm as you rage against the inequality we face, it means that you are human and that you care. Your generation of young women and feminists have to find a way to forge a new sisterhood, to support each other through the battles ahead. You don't have to just smile and look nice, you can also be a serious person, with serious intent.

Over the years, I have kept a very fat file of papers and newspaper cuttings for you. Even the small number that I have been able to include here, demonstrate the change in attitudes in the past thirty years. There is no doubt that in terms of personal politics Scotland at least is a much more progressive place. Yet the same tedious articles are written again and again about the tension between career and motherhood. Statistics now record that the average age of first time mothers has risen to thirty and the current head of the HFEA has a warning for women. *'Don't bank on IVF'.* Then Kirsty Allsopp (posh purveyor of posh houses) was savaged in the press and social media for daring to suggest women have children at a younger age. She said: *"Nature is not a feminist, do whatever you want but be aware of the fertility window. Make your choices in an informed way. This has been a taboo topic. People have not discussed it."* Really, Kirsty, where have you been? You need to get out more and read more feminist books. But that furore, in July 2014, correctly concluded that there is no template for being successfully female.

Your generation of young women has the world at your feet. But your destiny is very much in your own hands – without any template. Please, always try to find the courage needed never to acquiesce in your own oppression. Generations of women have fought hard to secure the rights that you now enjoy, to vote, to study, to travel, to work and to have or not to have babies.

You have the right to become a mother if you so wish, in whatever circumstances you choose. Wedlock doesn't come into it these days. Reproductive medicine and technology have hugely improved since my day. But you, and only you, can decide in which order you want to make your own life choices. Recent statistics also record a 15% increase in the number of

209

women becoming mothers over the age of forty. It is hard to know whether these women had fertility problems, had yet to meet a partner or wanted to have their career established before motherhood. But it is a worrying trend as fertility declines so rapidly after thirty. Look at my experience: these statistics don't tell us about the women who waited and then did not manage to become mothers at all. I know from my own failed cycles and from the experience of my circle of friends, the sadness which flows from late pregnancy and miscarriages which then no one acknowledges. Is motherhood now even harder?

If you do want to be a mother, darling, then please do think about it early, while you are young and healthy, young enough to fully appreciate the wonder of your children and while you have their feminist granny waiting in the background. Putting motherhood off to satisfy some mediocre boss, to purse your career or because you have no money are all completely spurious reasons to jeopardise what can be the most wonderful experience of your life. You can always go back to studying, you can work harder and change careers but you cannot always control your fertility. It will be hard, of course. But if you are prepared, it can also be wonderful.

If you choose not to become a mother, that is fine too. As long as it is really your choice and you take the time you need to think about and consider your reproductive options. During the last twenty-five years reproductive medical technology has advanced to the stage where young women are now being offered the chance to freeze their eggs, to delay motherhood to a more convenient time. I read these most recent articles with a mixture of dismay and fascination. How things have changed in such a short time? If employers are offering to pay for egg freezing for female employees then this surely opens up the possibility of more single mothers by choice, unless unlawful conditions were then placed upon accessing the frozen eggs only if you were married, in a partnership, etc.

Yet it is not forward thinking in my mind to encourage women to delay motherhood only to advance a career. In the end, the patriarchy would still be dictating your ability to become a mother – not the church and not the state – women shall decide their fate – and certainly not the bosses!

Chapter 24

I have struggled with how best to tell you all this. What you have read is the full adult version of the story I started as a picture book when you were two. Initially, I did not really want to look back. The very last thing I wanted to do was scribe a misery memoir because on the whole we have been far from miserable. Mostly, I have been angry and determined. Admittedly, there have been very difficult events and some episodes which sadly remain censured. Looking back has been both challenging and painful.

My biggest regret was not being able to have another child, that you have no full brothers or sisters. The doctors can provide no explanation for the unusual behaviour of my disappearing and reappearing exploding ovaries. While finishing this story, I came across an article in the Scotsman newspaper earlier this year under the headline: *Pregnancy drug women urged to claim pay-outs*. An American lawyer is encouraging DES daughters like me to claim compensation for fertility problems caused by this drug. Curious, I logged onto the website and read about the ovarian cysts and multiple failed IVF cycles experienced by thousands of women. This may be the answer that British doctors have yet to find out but I have not decided what steps to take other than to be very vigilant about my health, as I want to be around for many years yet.

You want to know more about your donor and understandably you want to satisfy your curiosity. As you want this story told to a wider audience, it is likely to now affect your life, much more than my own. I am by now a hardened old feminist with extremely thick skin. Tough as old boots, that's me. The most important thing in my life is your wellbeing, my one and only child.

Fertility treatment and trying to have a child took over more than a decade of my life. It has taken me another decade to write this story. Bringing you into this world and keeping you safe and well during these past two decades has, beyond all doubt, been my most important achievement.

My biggest fear was always that something would happen to me before you reached adulthood. As a result, I have probably been the most insured single parent ever. For the past few years, especially since Elliott died in 2007, I have wanted to wrap you in cotton wool and keep you safe, right by my side. But you have had other ideas. Besides Kenya, your back packing trips produced nerve racking calls from Prague, when the cash machine ate your bank card and you had no money, and Bulgaria when you and your pal got on the wrong train and were travelling in the wrong direction halfway across Serbia.

The saddest moments of my journey have been letting go of your embryonic brothers and sisters. Most tragic of all was scattering Elliott's ashes on a Vancouver beach. Such a beautiful boy, a credit to his heartbroken mother, full of energy and creativity but lost in a moment of teenage madness as he wanted to speed into adulthood. Many years have passed since then but still it is raw. Still so unbelievable, with repercussions every day for all who loved him. Your baby pictures are all with a wee boy who never became a man.

Your journey as a young adult has begun full of ambitions and adventures. You want to explore the world and look beyond the confines of our small family to explore the unknown, the unknown half of your genetic heritage. You have already taken steps on that journey writing an excellent article published in The Family section of the Guardian in February 2013. You were brave to write it and even braver to face down some of the more extreme internet comments and the offensive questioning and stereotypical assumptions of radio hosts. You want to embark on a new journey and I will support you every step of the way.

I want to help you, but also to protect you from hurt and disappointment. Yet that is impossible. I hope for your sake that another chapter is about to unfold and that whatever happens

213

your character will see you through. You may meet those five special people with a biological connection to you, or in time you may make connections with others and create new special people. It all lies before you and you have the right to follow your own path whatever it might be and wherever it may lead.

My advice to you is to embrace life, be determined to go after it all but always respect and acknowledge the struggles and achievements of generations of women before you. It may not be easy and things may not work out as you plan. Your destiny and your happiness are in your hands.

As you step out into the world my focus now has to shift from you, my child, to my mother. For a special treat we had champagne afternoon tea for Mother's day and I hope she will be there smiling proudly when you graduate.

Natasha and Mum on Mother's day

Mothers and daughters need each other at all ages and stages of life. As I grow into my sixth decade and my mother reaches her ninth, it is my turn to repay all the care and hard work, to look back, appreciate and understand her struggles much better than I did when I was twenty. In recent years, we have explored the Scottish Islands together, enjoying bowls of soup by day and gin and tonics by night and we have made peace with our old battles. She is slowing down, but her eyes light up when she sees you.

Once in charge of a whole hospital at night with clip-clopping court shoes, fitted blue uniform dress, and white nurse's hat secured to immaculately dyed and fashionable hair, your seventy-eight year old Nana now gets very cross when we try to tell her she is struggling to put a double duvet into a single cover. Sadly, forty years of constant night shift as a nurse have taken their toll.

We all noticed a difference in the past few years. My mum, who spent her life in the hairdresser, just can't be bothered anymore. She sometimes lets me get out the curling tongs but mostly she says, '*I am an old lady now, leave me alone.*' Cantankerous and still determined she cleans, washes and irons daily like her mother taught her. Being house proud was an important lesson drummed into generations of women like her. If she wants to go shopping, she demands that my dad drops everything as she gets her coat, hat and stick to head to Lidl's for the latest bargain. It is an aspect of her rarer form of dementia that she can become focussed on wanting something to happen immediately.

Most recently, your frail elderly grandmother gave us all a real fright. Without a word to anyone she took off on her own from Motherwell to her holiday flat in Millport on the Isle of Cumbrae because, as it turned out, she wanted two pillows. This journey involved three buses and a ferry which she managed on her own. But she never arrived at the flat. She was missing for eight hours and no one could contact her at the flat or on her mobile phone. Desperate with worry, and following his instincts that she was on her way to Millport, my dad tried to contact the one police officer based on the island. Alas, Police Scotland must have formal protocols to follow when someone reports an elderly person with dementia missing on an island. Helicopters were scrambled, the good folk of Millport went on Facebook and organised a search, the police checked CCTV cameras at Buchanan Street Bus Station in Glasgow as well as visiting the house in Motherwell to take a full statement from my dad and to check the shed. I didn't find out about this drama until very late in the day, as my dad did not want to worry me. Wrong call, as he now understands.

Thankfully, Mum turned up cold and hungry after dark at 9 o'clock at night, having managed the opposite journey on three buses and a ferry. She had the flat keys but couldn't manage to open the door, so turned and made her way home again to Motherwell. She wasn't bothered about the presence of the police in her living room, telling them proudly that she had used her bus pass, so her bid for freedom had been entirely free. Then she set about offering the police officers tea and macaroni cheese as she said she was starving, did they want some? So a new chapter has opened for our family involving power of attorney, vigilance and care.

How could I continue as a lawyer fighting every day for other women's rights and not help to look after my own mum in her old age? Not an easy question to answer as my award winning law firm employs eight other legal and admin staff. But decisions will have to be made and soon. Reading earlier chapters in this story and looking at photos of Nana with you as a baby, I know how much I owe her. It will be difficult, but the next stage for me must involve working less and making time for my mum when it matters when we have time still, to argue about doing her hair.

I am relieved that you are now grown up. We are waiting to see if you will move to London next year to do a masters degree in Social Policy. More than any previous generations of our family, the world will indeed be at your feet. Earlier this year I bought you a bookmark with the saying: "*Go confidently*

216

in the direction of your dreams." On the reverse I want to add the quote from Hilary Mantel. *"Don't be patronised by some talentless prat in a nylon shirt."*

This story is for you. I hope it helps to equip you for your battles ahead. I needed to write it all down so that you can set out on the next part of this journey with a full understanding of what went before.

I want to support you so that you can come to terms with our story in your own way, especially if the next stage of this journey ends in disappointment, especially about finding your donor and four half siblings. Life is full of challenges, joys as well as disappointments. Try as much as you can to focus on the positives, believe in yourself and you will not go far wrong.

When asking you some questions about dates for this book you sent me a text back. It said:

'You're a handful as a mother. You realise that right? You should put that in the book.'

And so I have. Giving you the last word, as you take our story forward into the chapters to come.

With all my love,

Your feminist mum.

Published in the Guardian Saturday 23 February 2013

Who is my sperm donor father?

by Natasha Fox

Natasha Fox was born by assisted donor conception to a single mother – a rarity in the early 90s. Nearly 21, she's had an insatiable curiosity since her early teens about the man who provided half her genes – and fears she'll never know

I've stopped calling him my father – he's my donor.

When I started school at five years old I didn't quite understand how I had come to be. I knew I was a result of assisted conception due to fertility treatment in London. My circumstances resulted from my mum's desire to have a baby as a single woman. She was refused treatment in Scotland because she wasn't married and moved to London to seek help.

I had been told stories and given information from a young age. However, as a child, not understanding the science behind my conception coupled with a vivid imagination, I convinced myself that I was a robot: a prospect that both scared and excited me. I knew I was special, as my mum had repeatedly told me.

She was open with me so I was never ashamed or shy about explaining that mine was a single-parent family. I thought it was only polite to be honest with the rest of the world: "It's just me and my mummy because the doctor helped make me," I'd say proudly.

At only five I was unable to process my mother's struggle to beat the odds against her uncooperative ovaries and the social stigma of wanting to become a single parent. Instead, what upset me most was that after numerous operations, she was unable to pick me up and swing me round like the dads who collected their daughters from school. Later on, at seven, I loved the occasional spotlight of attention at school, greeted with a surprise "oh" and smile from the teachers when I told them or when they saw my photograph in the newspapers. My primary teachers were understanding when it came to projects such as our family tree, and when the class made Father's Day cards I made cards for my mum or my grandpa.

I remember the day the headmaster approached me in the hallway, holding the newspaper that showed me and my mum smiling. He was full of praise.

I felt just as special as the kid who could run fastest in the class. At that age, I confidently retold stories of my mother's malfunctioning ovaries and numerous fertility treatments, which I, of course, considered to be a normal subject of conversation. I soon found out, however, that others did not hold the same view.

At a family wedding, another guest seated at our table innocently inquired about my dad. I launched into a long explanation of fertility treatment, sperm donors and single parenthood. When I had finished, the woman's face was the colour of her bright pink wedding hat and she was staring into her soup. My mum, sitting beside me, smiled when she caught the woman's eye and said, "Well, you did ask."When the subject of sex education came up at school, just before my 11th birthday, I raised my hand to remind the teacher that sex was not the only way to make babies.

During most of my primary years, I was unfazed by my lack of a father. But at 12, when I started secondary school, the issue came into sharper focus. Suddenly I had to deal with stronger, deeper emotions I had been too young to appreciate. What had made me special now brought me pain and sadness. My longing for a father-daughter relationship grew.

Mum and I talked about what my father might look like. What I treasured most was her saying, "At least you know he must be a very kind person."

She often joked that he must be messy because that was a trait I certainly did not get from her. I had an artistic streak she was baffled by and an interest in theatre. As a young teenager, I had seen nearly every musical on the West End stage and knew all the classics and Disney songs by heart – The Lion King was my favourite.

I constantly imagined meeting my father and fantasised that he must be searching his long-lost daughter. I also envied friends' relationships with their dads.

At 14, at my insistence, my mum wrote to the Human Fertilisation Embryology Authority (HFEA) and it provided the basic characteristics of my other biological parent. "Medium height, medium build, brown eyes, 5ft 6in", describing himself as "bright, chatty and extrovert", interests "arts and theatre", occupation "theatre director and manager". I was ecstatic. These bare facts made him feel real to me. He wasn't a figment of my imagination – he was out there.

At 15, I was less concerned about being special than fitting in. Close friends knew about my unconventional beginnings and were very accepting. Yet I felt I always put on a brave face and when people did ask, I used my stock phrase "test-tube baby", quickly dismissing with a smile and a "yes, isn't it interesting?" nod. I was less open because I didn't want to have to deal with the emotions that lay below the surface.

The information of a year earlier did nothing to stem my curiosity as my mum had hoped. If anything, it whetted my appetite for more. I longed to know who he was, to find out more now that I had something to build on. But Mum put her foot down. She felt I was too young to try to find him; we would do it when I was older.

These years were difficult for us both. I resented her for holding me back. I knew she was trying to protect me but from my adolescent perspective it felt like Mum was deliberately hurting me. I felt utterly alone.

She tried her best to help – she got in touch with the Donor Conception Network and arranged a meeting in London. Later on, I signed up to the Donor Sibling Registry based in the US, only to be met with false hopes.

When I was nearly 18, I was finally able to apply to the HFEA for more information. I had to send copies of my birth certificate and passport and Mum had to legally verify all the documents, which she could as she's a solicitor. Shortly afterwards, to my surprise and delight, the HFEA replied, informing me that I had four half-siblings – two girls and two boys – born in 1992 and 1993.

To an only child, finding out I was one of five ... it was much more than I could ever have hoped for.

Until my four half-siblings sign up to the voluntary registry I am not allowed to know anything about them – no name, no basic information, no contact details, nothing. The ball is in their court. I hope that my biological half-brothers and sisters share my curiosity. I also realise they may not be like me – maybe they have brothers and sisters, and maybe they don't know how they were conceived.

It was, at least, a comfort to know they were out there, like my dad, but, more than two years on, I am still waiting patiently for contact.

As I grew in confidence and maturity, I chose to stop my "fatherlessness" defining me. I stopped calling him my father and instead referred to him as my donor.

Now, in my second year of university in Edinburgh, I see things from a different perspective. I am not looking for my donor to be my dad any more but remain curious about who he is as a person. Does he know that he helped to bring five assisted-conception babies into the world? Perhaps he also has natural children of his own.

I want to know more about my donor and half-siblings but am unsure how best to turn my curiosity into reality. I'll be 21 this year and, rather than waiting, I hope this article might help me to make contact with an interesting theatre director and four half siblings. I am also curious to know if other people have similar stories to mine and are willing to share them. You never know, my donor might just be reading this newspaper.

Epilogue

Writing this story has been an all-consuming project, taking up very many weekends and holidays over very many years. I have received interesting support from the most unexpected quarters. I owe a great deal of thanks to a large number of people, most especially to my daughter and my parents. Without Simone too, I would not have been able to move to London to have fertility treatment and those early days with Elliott and Natasha in Hackney hold such precious, poignant, memories.

Entering the world of writing courses and meeting authors has been an exciting new direction and my heartfelt thanks go to Gillian Slovo and, most especially, to Frances Wilson who encouraged me in sisterhood to finish this story and not to hold back on the feminist rants. Thanks to my editor Isobel Freeman, who has guided this final manuscript to completion. By a fortuitous quirk of fate, my friend Maxine who helped to get me to hospital the second time had the connections over twenty-five years later to see this book published. Immense thanks are due to very many people and it seems fitting that this story will be published by Ringwood, a small independent publisher based in Glasgow. This is a Scottish story with barely any mention of football – a new genre perhaps?

I have finished this volume as a present to my daughter. I hope there will be a sequel in the near future. Her own full biological history has yet to fully unfold. The four half siblings discovered in 2010 have not yet made contact and may never do so unless they, too, are told their story and know of their assisted conception. This book might help. Natasha remains curious and hopeful. Her determination to find them and find out the identity of her donor remains undimmed and she has started to tell our story from her perspective from the Guardian to more recently, Closer Magazine.

When we moved back to Scotland from London in 1996, we went back often for weekends to visit friends and to see shows at Christmas and birthdays. She loves all the musicals and as a child would sing her head off in the car to all the Disney songs, the Lion King and Pocahontas. She certainly didn't inherit that from my Scottish ancestry. *'Wouldn't it be funny,'* I said to her one day, *'if your theatre director donor was there when we went to see the musical of the Lion King in London'*. *'Oh don't be so cheesy,'* was her exasperated reply but then I smiled back and told her that she should never close her mind to life's extraordinary possibilities.

It is a very true saying that what doesn't kill you makes you stronger. These previous chapters of my life have only served to make me more determined than ever to fight the feminist corner. Now that I am over fifty, and have no time to waste, I have developed zero tolerance towards any dithering, half measures. No more little miss nice person, I say. Over ten years ago to add to my collection of medical misfortunes, I was diagnosed with an underactive thyroid and was advised that one serious side effect of the daily thyroxin pills could include 'excitability'. Hell, I thought, I'd better broadcast a warning of some sort as most people think I am quite excitable enough *without* the medication.

In this book, I chose not to examine the mysteries of how my solidly conventional parents produced a toddler feminist and budding boy Marxist. All they really wanted was to work hard, give us both a good education and the best possible start in life. Instead, they produced an unconventional pair. Sometimes, life just deals you a hand, and perhaps even a child, that you do not expect. Sometimes, it just doesn't, no matter how hard you try. All any of us can do is to take what comes our way and do our very best in return.

That is what I have tried to do and I hope in writing it all down other mothers and daughters, especially, will take time to appreciate each other. God knows there are not enough

222

positive books out there about motherhood and too few that celebrate the wonders and strength of feminism. I hope that in years to come maddening radio phone in shows about mothers feeling eternally guilty will be replaced by positive celebrations of our achievements and our pride in our children.

I raise a glass to families everywhere, in all their shapes and sizes, as we keep going despite grief and disappointments, adversity and inequality, financial struggles and uncertainty. Most people struggle on day to day with humanity, determination and humour.

In finally reaching the end of this part of our story, I embrace my only daughter. I think of Elliott every day, and I salute, with immense gratitude, all working mothers and single parents, in all our varied circumstances, as we try to do our very best by our children.

Bibliography

A short history of the means of reproduction

"The joyful process of engendering a child, the patience of gestation, the fortitude to bring it into life, and the feeling of profound amazement with which everything culminates can be compared only to creating a book. Children, like books, are voyages into one's inner self, during which body, mind, and soul shift course and turn toward the very centre of existence."

Isabel Allende - **Paula**

The following books, written over the past three decades, record the lived experience of many women from very different perspectives. I read these feminist books for emotional sustenance and intellectual support during my battles with the medical establishment, during my many failed cycles and elusive quest for motherhood and again much later when I was making sense of being an unconventional single parent. I was so happy and so proud to be a mother, reading these books made be very grateful for the joy I experienced and proud of the choice I had made. Sadly, mine is not the universal experience, these honest feminist accounts do not promote any rosy view of motherhood, so be warned.

Adrienne Rich in *Of Woman Born* writes that "... *only the willingness to share private and sometimes painful experience can enable women to create a collective description of the world which will be truly ours."* As an academic, Rich wanted to write a history of motherhood based on her own experience. In the very first paragraph she writes about "... *exquisite suffering, ambivalence, bitter resentment and raw edged nerves, despair at her failings and selfishness."* A mother in the 1950s she struggled with the isolation of motherhood and the lack of identity for women beyond motherhood. After having three sons she took the decision to be sterilised. She became a famous poet and feminist writer. In her final paragraph she calls for the institution of motherhood to be destroyed, not for motherhood itself to be abolished but to "... *release the creation and sustenance of life into the same realm of decision, struggle, surprise, imagination and conscious intelligence, as any other difficult, but freely chosen work.*" Rich who died in 2012 aged 82 wanted us to imagine "... *a world in which every woman is the presiding genius of her own body.*" I couldn't agree more.

Why Children? is a collection of eighteen chapters on motherhood by different women exploring the *"... knotty problem of choice"* to convey "... *the complexity and the deep personal significance of the decision whether or not to have children.*" The collection builds upon the work of Adrienne Rich as these women write "... *about this world and the courage it takes to make choices in it, the courage it takes to try to change it ... to encourage many women to look into themselves – and dare to imagine."*

In **From Here to Maternity**, Ann Oakley records the experience of sixty ordinary women to give an authentic account of first time motherhood. The blurb on the back states that most women are unprepared for the pain and shock of birth or for the hard, selfless and lonely work of looking after a baby but the compensation is the baby itself.

Going Solo is based on interviews with women in America, Britain and the Netherlands who had to become single mothers. Renvoize concludes that "... *without exception, all those who made the deliberate choice to go solo have loving, joyful and rewarding experiences of motherhood.*"

The same theme of conscious motherhood is explored in Jean Shapiro's ***A Child Your Choice: An Honest Everyday guide to the Pleasures and Pain of Motherhood.*** My copy of this book is now yellow with age and very well thumbed as I read, and reread, the experiences of other women who chose to become mothers.

At the same time I was also reading ***Mad to be a Mother***

225

which again contained stark interviews with women about the difficulties and horrors of motherhood, dissecting the myths and pressing for change. At least the chapters had interesting titles like: *Rock the cradle, Rock the Boat* and *Mad mothers – or a mad world*. This book (pulished in 1987) coined the phrase, 'closet mothers', because women at work were not allowed to let their domestic commitments interfere with paid work. How little things have really changed in the last twenty years? At least this book ends on an optimistic note, "*Motherhood connects us to the women of the past and to generations to come. Motherhood confirms our strength and creativity and affirms our faith in the future. We need the future to be one in which we can love and enjoy our children because they are – for many of us- the best and most cherished part of our lives.*"

The Mother Knot by Jane Lazzarre is "... *a powerful autobiographical account of a woman who cares desperately about the rights to life of women living daily with children.*" The blurb says that it will *"frighten people who don't like to have their myths messed with, but that a lot of others will breathe easier because of it."* Lazarre talks about the 'motherhood mystique' and I love her homage to Virginia Wolf, *"I learned that motherhood can be written about truthfully and poetically, that women's lives as well as men's can be used as a means to glimpse a bit of all human reality and that, as Virginia Wolf instructed, all of us who feel compelled to write, must write so that the great poet who is Shakespeare's sister will be born again, this time not to die in an unmarked grave, but to write her poetry.*'

The Rocking of the Cradle and the Ruling of the World by Dorothy Dinnerstein is a heavyweight book recognised as "*A classic of feminist psychological and political analysis.*" Dinnerstein argues, somewhat controversially, that, "... *until we can fully understand and change the process by which men and women collude to maintain the woman in the role of mother we shall perpetuate not only the injustice of women's oppression but the alienation and brutalisation of men that so*

226

perilously threatens our planet." The 2nd edition was written just after the Chernobyl nuclear disaster in Russia which gives her thesis some urgency. Dinnerstein does not adopt a feminist perspective and rather than asking questions about the position of women per se, she starts from her concern about the survival of human society. I found a very old bookmark for the tenth birthday of Women's Press at Chapter 8 so I must assume that I didn't get to the end of this book to read her conclusion, "*What specific form the project of sexual liberation will take next, and which people will be most active in carrying it forward, cannot be predicted.*" Indeed, but then I don't suppose Dinnerstein imagined that both men and women in the 21st century would spend so much time watching cooking programmes and bake-offs in some faux nod to equality. At least our efforts at Greenham Common and Faslane mean that her central concern for the destruction of the planet has not yet been realised.

Balancing Acts: On Being a Mother, edited by Katherine Gieve, contains thirteen chapters from individual women describing how they coped with paid work and motherhood, addressing the same "having it all" dilemma "*Many women who grew up in the 1950s and 1960s and started their working lives with the ground swell of the women's movement, whether part of it or not, have hoped to able to have children and also to be their own persons, earn their own living and play a part in the public world. It doesn't seem too much to ask.*" The first chapter is written by the lawyer and working mother Helena Kennedy where she states "*I know that the law will never do justice to women if progressive women are not in there fighting our corner, but in some hidden recess of my heart, I feel I am greedily wanting it all.*"

Whose Choice? Working Class Women and the Control of Fertility by Vivien Steel is a slim volume outlining a manifesto of reproductive rights for working class women. For me there is a very interesting critique in Chapter 4: *"Infertility treatment, Warnock and the new reproductive technologies",* challenging the screening of IVF patients, *"The decision to proceed or not should be that of the individual directly concerned."* I couldn't agree more. At the time when Steel was writing that chapter in November 1990 I was enduring my failed cycles at BPAS.

Feminist Mothers by Tuula Gordon is another anthology of women's experiences of motherhood but this time of feminist mothers written from a sociological perspective, examining the public and the private domains and the struggles of motherhood. One interviewee talks about *"Motherhood as obliteration and struggling for identity"* which echoes the themes of Rich. However, Gordon noted that "... *although the sense of obliteration as one aspect of having children was present in many women's responses, this sense did not relate so much to motherhood as to the experience of being with children, and in particular being at home for prolonged periods."*

Alone Together, Voices of Single Mothers by Jenny Morris and ***Soul Providers, Writings by Single Parents*** by Gil McNeil are two collections which give voice to the experiences of single mothers. ***Alone Together,*** published in 1992, the year my daughter was born, records that there were *"... well over one million single mothers in Britain."* So we might just be counted in this number? It is a "... *hard hitting and inspiring book that at last gives a voice to some of these mothers themselves, dramatically overturning public presentations of single mothers as uniformly poor, struggling, oppressed and unhappy."*. In ***Soul Providers,*** there is a chapter which, when I reread the yellow pages all these years later, brought tears to my eyes for a mother and son, Madeline and Ky, whose story so closely parallels that of Simone and Elliott. Ky born in 1974 and died at 16 following an accident in Canada in 1990, the same year Elliott that was born.

What about us? An Open Letter to the Mothers Feminism Forgot by Maureen Freely is described as "... *a fury-driven attack on feminism, a raging at the sisters of the movement,*

228

who she feels, have betrayed her badly." Freeley asks "... have *we failed feminism or – to echo the classic backlash slogan – has feminism failed us?"* Freeley's conclusion is an uplifting call to women not to be fobbed off. She says *"I'm tired of being fobbed off with the long view. It's too much like being fobbed off with the promise of an afterlife. Ideas don't just happen. If you want them to prevail, you've still got to fight for them. You still have to make yourself heard, even if it's not the right climate. You've got to force them to acknowledge that there is a gap between the life they think you lead and the life you do live, the symbol they see and the woman you are. This is not a departure from feminism, but a completion of the original idea."*

The Parent Trap by Maureen Freely looks at the debates on parents, children and families over the twenty years of her parenting. She concludes that while life might have been much easier without four children she would not have experienced the joys children bring. *"Ask me if I have any regrets about having children, and you might as well be asking me if I've ever considered living without limbs, or what I imagine my life might be like if I'd never learned to read. Even today, with things so grim and getting daily grimmer, parents still talk about life with children as a joy."*

Will you be Mother?: Women who Choose to say No by Jane Bartlett is written from a very different perspective addressing the social pressures on women to become mothers and the advances in contraception which enable women to be child free. The chapters examine the experience of women "... *saying 'no' to childbearing and child raising – a high price to pay, some mothers may think. But to the child-free, all the elements of life to which they have said 'yes' are highly prized, and although some may have regrets and acknowledge ambiguities, others feel totally fulfilled. All of them would agree that what is important is that they are free to make that choice."*

Madonna and Child: Towards a new politics of Motherhood by Melissa Benn examines the political and social context of motherhood. She wanted to write her book because in the 'making it' culture she sensed *"... that women's more private, complex knowledge and experience of motherhood had somehow been driven underground."* In her concluding chapter entitled 'The Best of Both Worlds' she records "... *the most important feminist lesson of the last thirty years has been that the so called natural division of labour is really about a range of skills that can be shaken up and redistributed by those who have a will to do it."* I found a postcard from Melissa at the back of her book dated 1st August 2000 which she sent to me in response to my letter telling her how much I enjoyed her book. Melissa advocates 'Having less of it all' so that parenting and paid work are shared more equally, not just between men and women but between the better off and the poorest in society. She rails against what she calls 'bourgeois feminist triumphalism' typified by the likes of Nicola Horlick (high flying banker and mother of eight children) arguing that equality should not mean a few women having a lot more of what a few men had: power, fame and money but should mean "... *a greater economic and moral parity between all or citizens."*

Taking these books from my shelves twenty years later makes me wonder why we have stopped imagining a better future and fighting for change? Who is rocking the boat now? Who is speaking for mothers about our real experiences and shouting to be heard above the assumptions that it is all too difficult? Who truly believes that we live in a post-feminist world?

Why are more women than ever having babies over forty? Why are we retreating from having it all, or even less of it all?

What has happened to the feminist legacy outlined in these books and the struggles of these women, their courage to be mothers and to want to change the world?

My generation might be weary and exhausted needing some time out but the next generation of younger women, would be mothers and the child free, need to pick up the feminist baton. With a serious purpose and a serious intent to live full lives and make choices founded upon the hard won rights of their mothers and grandmothers.

This much I do know, no priest, no doctor, no boss, and no politician will come along and hand you the life you want.

In June 2013 it will be exactly one hundred years since Emily Wilding Davies threw herself under the King's horse in the Epson Derby fighting for women's suffrage. We need to embrace and celebrate our history and our own achievements. By the sheer rage and determination of women over the past century, our daughters have greater choices and opportunities than ever before. Our rights have been hard won and need to be fiercely protected.

Those of us who have made a small contribution, who have tried to live our politics and unapologetically demanded change, have played our part. Yet if we don't record our achievements for ourselves and our children how can they benefit from our struggles?

Who records feminist history, the changing politics of motherhood and the struggles of ordinary women and mothers who have children in all sorts of planned and unplanned circumstances and nevertheless keep the word turning?

With admiration for all those brave yet ordinary women that went before and, for those yet to come, this is my contribution – for my daughter – and all my sisters – past and present.

List of References

1. Memoirs

Allende, I.	(1996):	Paula.	Harper Collins.
Allende, I.	(2008):	The Sum of Our Days.	Harper Collins.
Angelou, M.	(1984):	I Know Why the Caged Bird Sing.	Virago.
Angelou, M.	(2008):	Letter to my Daughter.	Virago.
Blood, D.	(2004):	Flesh and Blood.	Mainstream.
De Beauvoir, S.	(1958):	Memoirs of a Dutiful Daughter.	Penguin.
Dickson, A.	(2012):	A Woman in Your Own Right	Quartet Books.
Galloway, J.	(2008):	This is not about me	Granta.
Galloway, J.	(2011):	All Made Up	Granta.
Hoffman, E.	(1989):	Lost in Translation.	Vintage.
Holmes, A.M.	(2007):	The Mistress's Daughter.	Granta.
Horlick, N.	(1997):	Can You Really Have It All?	MacMillan.
Johnson, S.	(1999):	A Better Woman.	Random House.
Johnstone, S.	(1989):	Hold on to the Messy Times.	Pandora Press.
Kay, J.	(2010):	Red Dust Road.	Picador.
Lessing, D.	(1995):	Under my Skin.	Flamingo.
Lessing, D.	(1998):	Walking in the Shade.	Flamingo.
Mantel, H.	(2003):	Giving Up the Ghost.	Fourth Estate.
McWilliam, C.	(2011):	What to look for in Winter	Vintage.
Moran, C.	(2011)	How to be a Woman?	Ebury Press.
Murray, J.	(2008):	Memoirs of a Not so Dutiful Daughter.	Bantam Press.
Segal, L.	(2007):	Serpent's Tail.	Virago.
Slovo, G.	(2007):	Every Secret Thing.	Virago.
Winterston, J.	(2001):	Oranges Are not the Only Fruit.	Vintage.
Winterston, J.	(2011):	Why be Happy When You Could be Normal?.	Vintage.

2. References for a 'Short History of Reproduction'

Allende, I.	(1996):	Paula.	Harper Collins.
Bartlett, J.	(1994):	Will You Be Mother?: Women Who Choose to Say No.	Virago.
Benn, M.	(1999):	Madonna and Child: Towards a New Politics of Motherhood.	Vintage.
Dinnerstein, D.	(1987):	The Rocking of the Cradle and the Ruling of the World.	Virago.
Freely, M.	(1995):	What About Us? An Open Letter to the Mothers Feminism Forgot.	Bloomsbury Publishing.
Freely, M.	(1990):	The Parent Trap.	Virago.
Gieve, K.	(1989):	Balancing Acts: On Being a Mother.	Virago.
Gordon, T.	(1990):	Feminist Mothers.	Macmillan.
Grundberg, S. and Dowrick, S.	(1980):	Why Children?.	The Women's Press.
Lazzarre, J.	(1987):	The Mother Knot.	Virago.
McConville, B.	(1987):	Mad to be a Mother.	Ebury Press.
McNeil, G.	(1994):	Soul Providers. Writings by Single Parents.	Virago.
Morris, J.	(1992):	Alone Together. Voices of Single Mothers.	Virago.
Oakley, A.	(1977):	From Here to Maternity.	Penguin.
Renvoize, J.	(1983):	Going Solo.	Routledge & Kegan Paul Books.
Rich, A.	(1977):	Of Woman Born.	Virago.
Shapiro, J.	(1987):	A Child of Your Choice.	Pandora.
Steel, V.	(1990):	Whose Choice? Working Class Women and the Control of Fertility.	Fortress.

3. Press coverage

Date	Publication	Title
15th Feb 1999	Daily Record	Labour's Test Tube Mum
16th Feb 1999	Daily Record	Make mine a double..
16th Feb 1999	The Times	IVF ambition of Labour hopeful
16th Feb 1999	Daily Mail	Hope of Unmarried Labour candidate
17th Oct 1999	Sunday Times	Women behaving disgracefully
31st Oct 1999	Scotland on Sunday	Last hope in bid to complete family
24th Sept2002	The Scotsman	Its the love that counts...
31st Aug 2004	Real Magazine	Celebrity single mums
16th July 2006	Scotland on Sunday	In the name of the Father
15th Dec 2006	The Scotsman	Way clear for access to IVF
23rd Feb 2013	The Guardian	Who's my sperm donor father?
16th Aug 2014	Closer Magazine	I worry I will never meet my father

Some other books from Ringwood Publishing

All titles are available from the Ringwood website (including
first edition signed copies) and from usual outlets.
Also available in Kindle, Kobo and Nook.
www.ringwoodpublishing.com

Ringwood Publishing, 7 Kirklee Quadrant, Glasgow, G12 0TS
mail@ringwoodpublishing.com
0141 357-6872

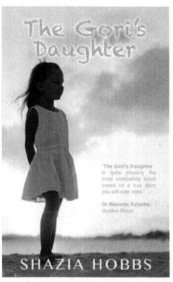

The Gori's Daughter

Shazia Hobbs

The Gori's Daughter is the story of
Aisha, a young mixed race woman,
daughter of a Kashmiri father
and a Glasgow mother. Her life is
a struggle against rejection and
hostility in Glasgow's white and
Asian communities.

The book documents her fight to
give her own daughter a culture
and tradition that she can accept
with pride. The tale is often
harrowing but is ultimately a
victory for decency over bigotry
and discrimination.

*"The Gori's Daughter is quite
possibly the most compelling novel
based on a true story that you will
ever read"* - **Dr Wanette Tuinstra -
Golden Room**

ISBN: 978-1-901514-12-4   £9.99

Torn Edges

Brian McHugh

Torn Edges is a mystery story linking modern day Glasgow with 1920's Ireland and takes a family back to the tumultuous days of the Irish Civil War.

They soon learn that many more Irishman were killed, murdered or assassinated during the very short Civil War than in the War of Independence and that gruesome atrocities were committed by both sides.

The evidence begins to suggest that their own relatives might have been involved

ISBN: 978-1-901514-05-6   £9.99

Silent Thunder

Archie MacPherson

Silent Thunder is set in Glasgow and Fife and follows the progress of two young Glaswegians as they stand up for what they believe in.

They find themselves thrust headlong into a fast moving and highly dangerous adventure involving a Scots radio broadcaster, Latvian gangsters, a computer genius and secret service agencies.

Archie MacPherson is well known and loved throughout Scotland as a premier sports commentator.

"An excellent tale told with pace and wit"

Hugh Macdonald -The Herald

ISBN: 978-1-901514-11-7   £9.99

Calling Cards

Gordon Johnston

Calling Cards is a psychological crime thriller set in Glasgow about stress, trauma, addiction, recovery, denial and corruption.

Following an anonymous email Journalist Frank Gallen and DI Adam Ralston unravel a web of corruption within the City Council with links to campaign against a new housing development in Kelvingrove Park and the frenzied attacks of a serial killer. They then engage in a desperate chase to identify a serial killer from the clues he is sending them.

ISBN: 978-1-901514-09-4   £9.99

A Subtle Sadness

Sandy Jamieson

A Subtle Sadness follows the life of Frank Hunter and is an exploration of Scottish Identity and the impact on it of politics, football, religion, sex and alcohol.

It covers a century of Scottish social, cultural and political highlights culminating in Glasgow's emergence in 1990 as European City of Culture.

It is not a political polemic but it puts the current social, cultural and political debates in a recent historical context.

ISBN: 978-1-901514-04-9   £9.99

Good Deed

Steve Christie

Good Deed introduces a new Scottish detective hero, DI Ronnie Buchanan.

It was described by one reviewer as *"Christopher Brookmyre on speed, with more thrills and less farce"*.

The events take Buchanan on a frantic journey around Scotland as his increasingly deadly pursuit of a mysterious criminal master mind known only as Vince comes to a climax back in Aberdeen.

ISBN: 978-1-901514-06-3   £9.99

Dark Loch

Charles P. Sharkey

Dark Loch is an epic tale of the effects of the First World War on the lives of the residents of a small Scottish rural community. The main characters are the tenant crofters who work the land leased to them by the Laird. The crofters live a harsh existence in harmony with the land and the changing seasons, unaware of the devastating war that is soon to engulf the continent of Europe.

The book vividly and dramatically explores the impact of that war on all the main characters and how their lives are drastically altered forever.

ISBN: 978-1-901514-14-8   £9.99